LATIN FOR
LOCAL AND FAMILY
HISTORIANS

1539.

A page from Burton upon Trent parish register, baptisms, 1539

LATIN FOR LOCAL AND FAMILY HISTORIANS

A Beginner's Guide

Denis Stuart

Phillimore

First published 1995
Reprinted 2000

Published by
PHILLIMORE & CO. LTD.,
Shopwyke Manor Barn, Chichester, West Sussex

ISBN 0 85033 984 7

Printed and bound in Great Britain by
Butler & Tanner Ltd, Frome and London

Contents

Acknowledgements

I am grateful to Dudley Fowkes, County Archivist, for general permission to use extracts from documents deposited in the Stafford County Record Office. Barbara Stuart commented critically on the text and has assisted in checking proofs and compiling the index and glossary. Christine Hanson of Phillimore has been of vital importance in determining the most effective lay-out for and the proof reading of a difficult text.

Introduction
Aims and Methods

This book is for adult students of local history and family historians who have no Latin and who consequently have not attempted to use Latin medieval and early modern sources in their researches. It aims to help the reader to acquire sufficient skill to translate the more commonly used and locally accessible documents in a field of study of which they may have been over-apprehensive. It does not seek to cover the whole range of primary source material nor to explain every grammatical irregularity or refinement of construction to be found, but it is sufficient for the beginner to make an effective start. The book is based on the belief that although Latin is not simple and cannot be made simple it is nevertheless manageable: the student who works conscientiously through this book will be equipped, and feel confident enough, to continue his studies for himself at a more advanced level.

A knowledge of Latin is necessary for local history and genealogical research up to 1733, when the act of 1731 came into force. Until that date (except for the period of the Commonwealth 1653-1660) Latin was the official language of most legal documents, including those produced at the local level. Without the ability to read documents written in Latin the local historian and genealogist is cut off from first-hand acquaintance with the vast bulk of early primary sources and restricted to material already translated or summarised and accessible. Two related skills are needed for dealing with the original material: first the ability to translate Latin and second the ability to read the older forms of handwriting. This book will help the beginner to acquire the first of these skills and also introduces the reader to an understanding of the abbreviations used by medieval scribes. With this equipment the reader will be able quickly and easily to acquire sufficient skill in palaeography to achieve his research purposes. There are plenty of comprehensive instruction manuals in reading the older forms of handwriting available, including that by the present author, *Manorial Records* (Phillimore, 1992).

Any new Do-it-Yourself textbook on this topic must owe much to Eileen Gooder's pioneer work *Latin for Local History* (Longman, 1961, revised edition 1978). The present book, like Gooder's, postulates that adults, like children, learn best by doing, and that the teacher's task is to facilitate the learning process as well as to instruct. It differs from Gooder, however, in a number of ways: it is more 'user-friendly' while retaining Gooder's high expectation of the user's perseverance and ability to grasp grammatical principles; the pace of instruction is slower and there is deliberately an element of 'drill' in the exercises; to promote familiarisation with the basic vocabulary of local history, commonly found nouns and verbs are repeated though in different cases and tenses; new words are at first only slowly introduced; there is instruction on how to consult and use a word list or dictionary for translation; in place of Gooder's formulary of documents there are special chapters which deal with the structure as well as the vocabulary of a range of documents including the simpler types of church or diocesan material used in local and genealogical research, manorial records, charters and deeds. These have been chosen for their intrinsic historical or genealogical interest as well as to illustrate points of grammar; brief explanations are occasionally added to provide background and assist further understanding of the extracts. The book contains all the tables of declensions and conjugations necessary for the translation of the exercises and there is no need for the student to refer to any other textbook. Passages for translation are at first short and carefully graded in difficulty so as to promote a growing sense of confidence; any constructions or unusual forms in the exercises and not previously explained are followed immediately by the relevant translation in brackets. Grammatical explanations deal with only one or two matters at a time and these are followed by exercises which immediately drive home the point. As soon as possible the exercises are based on extracts from real documents.

For the student who 'did some Latin at school', to acquire the facility to read medieval Latin will simply be a matter of brushing up the elementary grammar and noting that many of the niceties of the classical period are gone. If you are a beginner it is not necessary to memorise thousands of words; you work at your own pace, translating with your dictionary and textbooks beside you. After working through this book you will still not be able to read Caesar's *De Bello Gallico* at sight but you will have enhanced your skills as a local or family historian.

The differences between Classical and Medieval Latin
(Beginners can defer reading this section until after they have come to the end of Chapter 3.)

The medieval Latin of most documents of a local historical character is a simplified version of the classical language. It was much influenced by the *Vulgate*, the Latin Bible begun by St. Jerome in 382 A.D. The syntax, that is, the rules governing the grammatical arrangement of the words, is looser than in classical Latin, and the constructions are sometimes Anglicised. The most common medievalisms are:

- the use of the prepositions *de, ad* and *per* followed by a noun where classical writers would have had a simple noun with the appropriate case-ending
- the avoidance of an accusative and infinitive construction by the use of *quod*; thus *dixit Robertum probum esse* 'He said Robert was honest' (literally 'He said Robert honest to be') becomes in medieval usage *dixit quod Robertus probus erat*
- the greater use of the word *quod* 'that' in Anglicised constructions such as *proviso quod* 'provided that'

The main differences, however, lie in spelling. Variants include:

Classical	Medieval	Example	Meaning
-ae	-e	quae (que)	which
-oe	-e	coelum (celum)	heaven
-h-	-ch-	nihil (nichil)	nothing
-ti	-ci	gratia (gracia)	grace
-ct-	-cc-	exactio (exaccio)	demand
c-	-s-	concessio (consessio)	grant
-sc-	-ss-	nescio (nessio)	I do not know
ob-	op-	obtineo (optineo)	obtain
extra p		damnum (dampnum)	damages

These changes may not worry you as much as might variant spellings of the same word. For example the world 'assart', meaning a 'clearing in the wood', appears in medieval Latin texts in numerous forms—*assarta, essarta, exsarta, exsartum, sartum, acertum,* etc.

Medieval Latin documents also contain many words not found in a classical dictionary, e.g. *croftum* 'croft'. Local scribes had no hesitation in using Latinised English e.g. *shopa* 'shop'. A few classical words acquired different meanings, e.g. *miles* means 'knight' not 'soldier'.

Many of the documents that you will want to translate, such as deeds, manorial records, marriage bonds etc., are full of set patterns of words, verbal formulae known as 'common form' expressions, which you will soon recognise and which give you immediately something of the meaning of a document. Here are some examples:

> *Sciant presentes et futuri ...*   'Know, (i.e. all men) present and future ...'
> (This is a phrase which begins many deeds connected with the conveyance of property)

> *Curia tenta ...* 'The court held ...' (followed by a date)
> (A heading which begins many manor court rolls)

> *secundum consuetudinem manerii* 'according to the custom of the manor'
> (in manorial copyhold land transactions)

How to Use this Book

In learning to read Latin documents with the assistance of this book you will not be learning to speak a foreign language. Latin can be learned in a modern way in a language laboratory. This book simply provides the rules and a basic vocabulary sufficient to give you confidence to go still further in your pursuit of a special skill. The old-fashioned grammatical approach is used, but this is the best method of learning when you have to work alone. There is no need for apprehension about Latin grammar; it has only come to be regarded as an obstacle because few of us have been taught how our own language is constructed. In the first chapter of this book there are exercises to supply you with, or refresh your memory of, English grammatical terms. As for the Latin vocabulary, 40 per cent of English words are derived from Latin and you can guess correctly or deduce the meaning of many words from their English derivatives. Do not be persuaded by anyone that it is unnecessary to know much Latin to be able to research your own local material. The essentials of a document may be quickly obtained but the greater your command of grammar and vocabulary the wider will be the range of sources you will be able to explore.

It will be helpful to say the words aloud, but do not worry about pronunciation. Speak the letters as you would in English, making sure you sound all the consonants and vowels. For example *pateat* 'let it be known', is pronounced 'pat-ee-at', *regine* is not 're-jyne' but re-gy-nee'; 'c' and 'g' were hard in classical Latin, as in 'cat' and 'dog', but soft in medieval speech (as in modern church Latin); 'v' was sounded as a 'w' and Julius Caesar probably pronounced *Veni vidi vici*—'I came, I saw, I conquered'—as 'Wayny weedy weaky'. If you wish, look at the hints on pronunciation given in any good Latin grammar.

Work systematically through the text and the exercises, checking your answers as you proceed and revising frequently. As you translate try to account grammatically for the form taken by the endings of words, asking yourself why a particular ending has been used. The first twenty or so exercises require you to do this; the experience you will gain from this practice will be useful, indeed essential, when later on you have to extend the abbreviations found in actual documents.

If you are not an absolute beginner and already have some acquaintance with the types of document dealt with here you could try going straight to Chapter 4. If you find you are making grammatical mistakes you should refer back to the appropriate sections using the grammatical index to locate these. The index also refers to illustrations and examples of the main points of grammar as they occur in the extracts or documents used throughout the book.

Part 1
BASIC LATIN GRAMMAR

Chapter 1

Looking at Latin Grammar: Verbs and their Conjugation; Nouns and their Declension; Conjunctions; Adjectives and their Agreement; Prepositions and their Cases; Using the Glossary (Nouns)

The main grammatical difference between English and Latin is that in English the position of the word in the sentence will usually show how it is being used, whereas in Latin it is the ending of the word that indicates its function. The difference in meaning between 'Henry sees the farmer' and 'The farmer sees Henry' depends entirely on the position of the nouns 'Henry' and 'farmer' in relation to the verb 'sees'. In Latin the endings of the nouns would change; in the first sentence 'Henry' would be *Henricus* but in the second *Henricum*; 'farmer' would be *agricolam* in the first sentence, but *agricola* in the second. These changes in word endings take place in nouns, pronouns, adjectives and verbs and are called 'inflections'. Latin is a highly inflected language whereas English has lost most of the inflections that it once had. Not entirely: we say 'I saw the farmer' but we also say 'The farmer saw me'. Latin makes such changes to the endings of the words all the time. The stem of a word gives its basic meaning but the ending adds a special meaning. It is not the position of the word in the Latin sentence that is important but its ending. In Latin not only nouns but verbs change their endings; again English is not completely free from this: we say 'I see', 'You see', 'They see' but also 'He sees'. Look carefully at the endings of Latin words as well as the beginning.

Verbs are of two main sorts. TRANSITIVE verbs express an action which requires an object to complete its meaning: in 'The lord grants a charter' the word 'grants' requires an object 'charter' to complete the meaning; INTRANSITIVE VERBS complete the thought within themselves and do not require an object, e.g. 'The villein works'. As stated above Latin verbs have a stem which gives the general meaning, and an ending which adds a particular meaning. Thus *ara-* is the stem of the verb meaning 'to plough' and endings are added to this stem to show who is ploughing:

ar-o	I plough (really *ara-o* but the *a* has been lost)
ara-s	thou ploughest (you must use this singular form)
ara-t	he/she/it ploughs
ara-mus	we plough
ara-tis	you plough (plural)
ara-nt	they plough.

There is no PRONOUN 'he', 'we' etc. because this is understood from the ending of the verb. Of course the subject may be separately expressed

arat   he ploughs   *agricola arat*   the farmer ploughs.

Verbs express an action or state and in Latin fall into one of four main groups or CONJUGATIONS. There is also a mixed conjugation, and there are many irregular verbs. Each conjugation has its own characteristics: thus *aro* belongs to the first conjugation which is distinguished by the terminal *a-* of the stem. Another verb of this conjugation, *confirmo*, 'I confirm', a word frequently encountered in charters and deeds, conjugates similarly:

Singular		**Plural**	
confirmo	I confirm (i.e. a charter or grant)	*confirmamus*	we confirm
confirmas	thou confirmest	*confirmatis*	you confirm
confirmat	he/she confirms	*confirmant*	they confirm.

This is the form taken by the PRESENT TENSE or time. There are different endings for other tenses so the ending of a verb shows you not only the tense but also the PERSON (I, he, you, etc.), and the NUMBER (singular or plural).

Modern English has lost most but not all of the endings which Old and Middle English had. In the word 'plough' above, all the English forms are the same except for the third person 'ploughs' which retains a terminal 's' and we no longer employ the singular form 'ploughest'.

Exercise 1
Guess at the meanings of the following verbs, check from the Glossary, then write down the full conjugation of each verb in the present tense on the model of *aro* and *confirmo* above.

edifico, laboro, voco, assigno, contento

(Remember that in a classical dictionary you will find *aedifico*)

NOUNS are the names of persons, places, things and qualities, and like verbs they consist of an unchanging stem which gives a general meaning and an ending which changes to give a special meaning. Latin nouns are grouped into five declensions, the first declension being characterised by an *-a-* in most of the endings.

Exercise 2
Guess the meanings of the following nouns, then check your answers. (The point of this exercise is to demonstrate how often you can guess correctly at the basic meaning of a Latin word.)

*Roma, terra, luna, filia, insula, littera, vita, carta, parsona,
parochia, ecclesia, pastura, ropa, regina, Iulia*

(Note an initial *i* and *j* are interchangeable.)

Latin does not use the definite and indefinite articles 'the' and 'a'; you have to decide which is meant from the general context; thus *curia* means both 'the court' and 'a court'. In Latin there are six endings to nouns which give different meanings (although some of the endings are similar in form). English nouns used to have such changes, called, as we have seen, inflections, but has now lost nearly all of them. The different forms of the nouns are called CASES. Here are two examples of nouns of the FIRST DECLENSION which is characterised by -a- in the ending, (the hyphen between the stem and the ending is only for clarity at this stage).

Case		**Noun** (singular)		
Nominative	*regin-a*	queen	*cart-a*	charter
Vocative	*regin-a*	O queen!	*cart-a*	O charter!
Accusative	*regin-am*	queen	*cart-am*	charter
Genitive	*regin-e*	of a queen	*cart-e*	of a charter
Dative	*regin-e*	to (or) for a queen	*cart-e*	to a charter
Ablative	*regin-a*	by/with/from a queen	*cart-a*	by/with/from a charter

Which case-ending of the noun is used depends on its function in the sentence. The nominative case (i.e. ending) is used when the noun is the SUBJECT of the sentence, that is, the person or thing carrying out the action of the verb (ascertain this by asking 'Who?' or 'What?'); the accusative case is used for the DIRECT OBJECT of the verb, that is, the person or thing suffering or receiving the action. Thus in the sentence *Regina confirmat cartam* 'The queen confirms the charter', the subject of the sentence is 'Queen' so in Latin this is in the nominative case and the ending is -*a*; 'charter' is the direct object of the verb 'confirms', and must therefore be in the accusative case and so ends in -*am*. Here are six somewhat simplified rules showing how the six case-endings are used in Latin:

Rule 1   Nominative case for the subject of the sentence or clause *agricola arat* 'the farmer ploughs'
Rule 2   Vocative case to address someone (not often found in local history documents) *O Regina!* 'O Queen'
Rule 3   Accusative case when the noun is a direct object *agricola arat terram* 'the farmer ploughs the land'
Rule 4   Genitive case to answer question 'belonging to whom?' *parsona occupat terram agricole* 'the parson seizes the land of the farmer'
Rule 5   Dative case is used for an indirect object, i.e. the person to whom something is given, shown or told *terram agricole dat* 'he/she gives land to the farmer'. (Remember it is not the order of words that is decisive in Latin but the endings; there was no subject expressed in the sentence above but it was in the verb already. LOOK AT THE ENDINGS OF THE WORDS!)
Rule 6   Use the ablative case

(a)   with various prepositions to state place where *in terra* 'in the land *e* (or) *ex terra* 'out of the land'
(b)   with various prepositions to state place from whence *a* (or *ab*) *terra* 'from the land'

(c)   by itself to indicate the means by which something is done *regina agricole carta terram dat* 'the queen gives land to the farmer by a charter'

Here *carta* is in the ablative case although it looks the same as a nominative. No other translation would make sense. Note also a new first conjugation verb *dat*, from *do* 'to give':

do	I give (or) am giving
das	thou givest (art giving)
dat	he gives (is giving)
damus	we give (are giving)
datis	you give (are giving)
dant	they give (are giving)

There are numerous other occasions when the different cases must be used, but this will do for a start. You may by now be wishing you could remember more basic English grammatical terminology. The next exercise will refresh your memory.

Exercise 3
Pick out from the sentences below **nouns** (names of things or persons) 'queen', 'John'; **pronouns** (used in place of a noun), 'he', 'she', 'they' etc; **verbs**; **adjectives** (which describe a noun), 'red', 'good'; **adverbs** (which describe the action in a verb or qualify an adjective, 'slowly', 'not'; **prepositions** (which show relations between words), 'in', 'by', 'for'.

(a)   He surrendered the tenement into the hands of the lord.
(b)   The jury say he is not guilty.
(c)   The court was held on the Monday after the feast of Saint James.

The next exercise requires you to repeat this and also to state in what case the nouns would be in Latin. Follow this model:

'The king generously grants land in the parish of St. Michael to the church'

'The' definite article (not found in Latin)

'king' **noun** nominative (subject)

'generously' **adverb** (qualifying 'grants'; no changes in form)

'grants' **verb** (present tense, 3rd person, singular)

'land' **noun**, accusative (direct object)

'in' **preposition** ablative (connecting 'land' and 'parish')

'St Michael' **noun**, genitive (the 'of' or possessive form)

'to' **preposition** dative (joining 'grants' to 'church')

'church' **noun** (dative, INDIRECT OBJECT of 'grants', to whom the land is given)

Exercise 4
Identify the grammatical terms and state the case the nouns and pronouns would be in if they were in a Latin sentence.

(a) The lord readily grants a charter to the borough
(b) John Wodard comes into the court and does fealty
(c) He holds one acre of villein land in the manor of Berham
(d) By this charter we confirm the grant of tithes to the church
(e) The defendant unjustly raised (past tense) the hue and cry
(f) I affix my seal to the will.

To translate simple local history sentences, follow this procedure:

1. read the sentence aloud,
2. find the verb (often the last word in the sentence),
3. find the subject of the verb (either understood in the verb itself or a noun/pronoun in the nominative case),
4. find the direct object (if any) in the accusative case,
5. find the indirect object (if any) in the dative case,
6. find any words in the genitive or ablative case connected with some noun/pronoun,
7. put it together to make sense. Remember that when you translate you do not have to follow the order of the words as they appear in the Latin; add a definite or indefinite article if necessary. Here is an example:

Regina cartam puelle dat

a. Emphasise the endings to remind yourself of their importance.
b. Which is the verb? *dat* 'gives'.
c. What is the subject, that is, who is the sentence about? *Regina* 'queen'.
d. Does the verb have a direct object, that is, is there a noun in the accusative case necessary to complete the sense of the verb? What is the queen giving? *cartam* 'charter'.
e. Is there an indirect object, the person to whom something is given, and which is in the dative case? *puelle* 'to the girl'.
f. Nothing else in this sentence.
g. Add 'the' or 'a' as seems appropriate.

Exercise 5
Translate into English. (There are some notes and reminders to help you with what is perhaps your first ever Latin sentence.)

(a) *Regina parochie terram dat*
(b) *Rex parsone cartam dat*
(c) *Rex carta terram confirmat* (Careful! No indirect object)
(d) *Dominus terram ecclesie occupat* (The sense tells you what is the case and therefore what is the correct translation of *ecclesie*)

(e)   *Vaccam puelle do* (Remember the order of the words in a Latin sentence is not decisive; note that the subject of this sentence is contained in the verb and is not expressed separately)

(f)   *In parochia dominus habet* (holds) *acram terre* (Note the ablative case indicating place where after the preposition *in;* the verb is not at the end of the sentence this time)

CONJUNCTIONS are words which join words or sentences together. The following are simple connectives which do not affect the case of the nouns they join, but there are others which require changes in the verbs which follow.

et	and
et ... et	both ... and
aut	or
aut ... aut	either ... or
nec (or) *neque*	neither
neque ... neque	neither ... nor
sed	but

In Latin the absolute beginner must know what he is doing and not merely translate as if learning a language in the modern way, with little or no grammar to begin with. Accordingly all the passages for translation in this and the next chapter now require you to state the case and number of the nouns, as in the following example:

Agricola terram in parochia parsone dat

The farmer gives land in the parish to the parson.

Agricola (nom.sing.) *terram* (acc.sing.) *parochia* (abl.sing.) *parsone* (dat. sing.)

Exercise 6
Translate stating case and number of the nouns.

(a)   *Dominus cartam neque dat neque confirmat*

(b)   *Et parsona et dominus pasturam in terra habent* (have or hold)

(c)   *Parsona vaccam et terram filie agricole dat* (the sense will indicate to you what is the case of the two nouns *filie* and *agricole*, which have a similar ending in *-e*, and therefore what the translation must be).

PLURAL (more than one) noun endings differ from the SINGULAR.

	Singular	**Plural**	*acra* 'acre' (1st Declension)
Nom.	*acra*	*acre*	(terminal *-a* changes to *-e*)
Voc.	*acra*	*acre*	(terminal *-a* changes to *-e*)
Acc.	*acram*	*acras*	(*-m* changes to *-s*)
Gen.	*acre*	*acrarum*	(note the ending *-rum* of gen. pl.)
Dat.	*acre*	*acris*	(the endings of dat. and abl.pl. are the same)
Abl.	*acra*	*acris*	

Study this model translation of plural forms

Agricole puellis terras dant (plural verb 'give')

The farmers give lands to the girls

Agricole (nom.pl.) *puellis* (dat.pl.) *terras* (acc.pl.)

Exercise 7
Translate stating case and number.

(a) *Rex ecclesiis terras dat*
(b) *Dominus terras agricolarum occupat*
(c) *Julia filia parsone tenementum* (tenement) *cum ij acris terre habet* (The first two nouns are in APPOSITION, that is, the second noun, in the same case as the first, follows and describes it; the preposition *cum* must be followed by an ablative case; in the medieval version of the Roman numeral 2 the last MINIM—a single down stroke of the pen—is usually written as a—*j*)

Exercise 8
Translate these nouns then write down the singular and plural forms of the six case-endings of the first two

filia*, vacca, carta, pastura, bosca, curia, villa, fossa

*see answer for an irregularity in the declension of this noun.

Exercise 9
Translate

(a) *Nos, rex et regina, terras ecclesie occupamus*
(b) *Dominus e gracia cartam ecclesie confirmat*
(c) *Quando cartam confirmatis?*
(d) *Quando parsone pecuniam contentas?*
(e) *Ecclesia unam acram in parochia habet*

Another group of nouns belongs to the SECOND DECLENSION. We have seen one of these already—*dominus*—meaning 'lord'. Here is the full declension.

Note how the endings differ from the form of (mostly) feminine nouns of the first declension.

dominus (m.) 'lord', 'Sir' (courtesy title for cleric), judge

	Singular	**Plural**	**Use**
Nom.	*dominus*	*domini*	subject/s of the verb
Voc.	*domine*	*domini*	in exclamations or greetings
Acc.	*dominum*	*dominos*	object/s of the verb
Gen.	*domini*	*dominorum*	possession, 'of the lord/s'
Dat.	*domino*	*dominis*	the 'to' or 'for' case
Abl.	*domino*	*dominis*	the 'from/by/with/in' case

There are two other models in this declension to observe

magister (m.) 'master'

	Singular	Plural	Use
Nom.	*magister*	*magistri*	(the stem retains 'r' and 'e' is lost
Voc.	*magister*	*magistri*	except in Nom. and Voc.)
Acc.	*magistrum*	*magistros*	(-*um* becomes -*os*)
Gen.	*magistri*	*magistrorum*	(note the gen.pl. -*rum*)
Dat.	*magistro*	*magistris*	(dat. and abl. have same plural form
Abl.	*magistro*	*magistris*	as 1st decl.)

The third type of noun in this declension is of neuter GENDER. By a grammatical convention Latin distinguishes between masculine (m.), feminine (f.) and neuter (n.) nouns. Most nouns of the first declension are feminine, most of the second are masculine but there are some, which end in -*um*, which are neuter (n.).

pratum 'meadow' (n.)

	Singular	Plural	Use
Nom.	*pratum*	*prata*	'meadow/s'
Voc.	*pratum*	*prata*	(note that the first three cases have
Acc.	*pratum*	*prata*	similar forms in singular and plural)
Gen.	*prati*	*pratorum*	
Dat.	*prato*	*pratis*	
Abl.	*prato*	*pratis*	

Exercise 10

Guess the meanings of the following second declension nouns, check your answers, then write out the full declension, both singular and plural, of the first three

annus, puer, messuagium, locus, regnum, campus, manerium

At this stage you will probably be spending a lot of time looking at the tables of the declensions and conjugations. If you are feeling slightly desperate *Nil desperandum!* (A quotation from a classical Latin author, Horace *Epistles*, 1,7 inserted here for light relief but also because we shall be meeting this construction later on!)

Exercise 11
Translate

(a) *Dominus manerii curiam habet*
(b) *Rex burgo cartam dat*
(c) *Servis pecuniam damus*
(d) *Nos, Robertus et Henricus, ecclesie Sancti Petri decem acras terre in parochia assignamus*
(e) *Virgatam terre ecclesie datis*
(f) *Terras filio Willelmi do et carta confirmo*

(g) *Dominus messuagia cum terris agricolarum in manerio occupat*
(h) *Senescallus pasturas et boscas villanis in manerio assignat*

It will be convenient to consider next the FOURTH DECLENSION because it has some endings similar to those of the second; and the two can be confused. Luckily neither the fourth nor the fifth declensions has many words.

FOURTH DECLENSION Model *manus* (f.) 'hand'

	Singular	Plural
Nom.	*manus*	*manus*
Voc.	*manus*	*manus*
Acc.	*manum*	*manus*
Gen.	*manus*	*manuum*
Dat.	*manui*	*manibus*
Abl.	*manu*	*manibus*

There is not so much change in form in this declension and the meaning has to be derived from the general sense of the passage. The word *manus* is frequently found in manorial court rolls in the entries dealing with the transfer of land held on copyhold tenure, where Tenant A legally had to surrender his land **into the hands**— *in manus domini*—of the lord who then granted it to Tenant B. Analysing this phrase we have, therefore

in	preposition which in this instance is followed by an accusative case not an ablative because here it means 'into' and denotes motion towards
manus	must be plural 'hands'
domini	'of the lord', the genitive case of possession

There is another model, of neuter gender, for this fourth declension, with the endings *-u, -u, -u, -us, -ui, -u* for the singular and *-ua, -ua, -ua, -uum, -ibus, -ibus* for the plural. Refer to the tables at the end of the book for this.

The fourth declension includes an important irregular noun, *domus* 'house' (f.)

	Singular	Plural	
Nom.	*domus*	*domus*	
Voc.	*domus*	*domus*	
Acc.	*domum*	*domos*	(sometimes *domus*)
Gen.	*domus*	*domuum*	(sometimes *domorum*)
Dat.	*domui*	*domibus*	
Abl.	*domo*	*domibus*	

Apart from *manus* and *domus* two other nouns of the fourth declension, often met in local historical documents, are *visus* (m.) meaning 'view' and *redditus* (m.) 'rent'. The word *visus* often appears in manor court rolls as the six-monthly court which checked that all male inhabitants of the manor were enrolled in a frankpledge or tithing, a group of ten households.

visus franciplegii tentus die Jovis ...
view of frankpledge held on Thursday ...

There are very few nouns in the FIFTH DECLENSION, the two most frequently found being:

	res (f.) 'thing'			*dies* (m.) 'day'	
	Singular	**Plural**		**Singular**	**Plural**
Nom.	*res*	*res*		*dies*	*dies*
Voc.	*res*	*res*		*dies*	*dies*
Acc.	*rem*	*res*		*diem*	*dies*
Gen.	*rei*	*rerum*		*diei*	*dierum*
Dat.	*rei*	*rebus*		*diei*	*diebus*
Abl.	*re*	*rebus*		*die*	*diebus*

These are the only nouns in this declension which have genitive, and ablative plural; all nouns in this declension are feminine except *meridies* 'noon' and *dies* which is masculine in the singular when it means 'an appointed day' (a rule not always observed).

consideratum est quod dictus Nicholaus habeat diem
it was decided that the said Nicholas may have a day
(i.e. his case would be heard at a later court)

datum die et anno supradicto
dated on the day and year above written

quo die apparuit et dominus monuit eum
on which day he appeared (i.e. in court) and the judge warned him.

These examples show that the ablative form *die* is used to express the time when something is done.

in cuius rei testimonium
in witness of which (thing)

Exercise 12
Translate and explain the case, number and gender of the nouns.

(a)   *Curia magna* ('great') *domini Henrici de Ferrers cum visu franciplegij ...*
(b)   *Visus franciplegij tentus* ('held') *in crastino Sancti Matthei ...*
(c)   *Parsona solvit* ('pays') *iij solidos redditum*

(d) *Ad hanc* ('this') *curiam venit* ('comes') *Willelmus Lathropp de Legh in comitatu Staffordie et sursumreddit* ('surrenders') *in manus domini manerij predicti* ('aforesaid') *medietatem duorum messuagiorum*
(e) *Ricardus de Potlak tenet unum burgagium et solvit abbati xijd*
(f) *Elena filia Walteri carpentarij tenet pratum iuxta Skyrem medwe* ('meadow', an English word found in a Latin rental of 1319)

Notice the terminal *j* in place of '*i*'

Adjectives

The previous exercise introduced two adjectives, 'great' and 'aforesaid'. Adjectives are words which qualify or describe a noun more clearly, e.g. 'a red rose'. They 'agree' with the noun they qualify; that is, they have the same gender, number and case. So in the exercise above *magna* described *Curia*, and was therefore nominative, feminine and singular; *predicti* described *manerij* and agreed with that noun, but this time the adjective was in the genitive case and was neuter and singular. Adjectives, because they agree with nouns, must similarly 'decline' and this they do either like feminine nouns of the first declension or masculine and neuter nouns of the second declension on the model of *bonus* 'good' below. (Third declension adjectives are dealt with later.)

	Feminine	Masculine	Neuter	Feminine	Masculine	Neuter
		Singular			**Plural**	
Nom.	*bona*	*bonus*	*bonum*	*bone*	*boni*	*bona*
Voc.	*bona*	*bone*	*bonum*	*bone*	*boni*	*bona*
Acc.	*bonam*	*bonum*	*bonum*	*bonas*	*bonos*	*bona*
Gen.	*bone*	*boni*	*boni*	*bonarum*	*bonorum*	*bonorum*
Dat.	*bone*	*bono*	*bono*	*bonis*	*bonis*	*bonis*
Abl.	*bona*	*bono*	*bono*	*bonis*	*bonis*	*bonis*

Rex ecclesie terras bonas dat

The king gives good lands to the church
bonas is accusative feminine plural agreeing with *terras*

Exercise 13
Translate and explain the case, number and gender of the adjectives.

(a) *Rex ecclesie terram bonam dat*
(b) *Dominus servo bono terras assignat*
(c) *Terra domini multas vaccas habet*
(d) *Dominus burgo predicto cartam confirmat*
(e) *Servis bonis pecuniam damus*
(f) *Dominus Willelmus terras parsone predicti occupat*
(g) *Nos, predicti Edwardus et Elizabetha, ecclesie Sancti Modwenne decem acras terre in manerio nostro assignamus*

PREPOSITIONS have already been mentioned in connection with Rule 6 concerning case-endings. Some prepositions are followed by a noun or pronoun in the ablative case. These include

in	in
coram	in the presence of
cum	with
de	of, from
pro	for
e or *ex*	out of
a or *ab*	from, by
sine	without

Some prepositions are followed by an accusative case. These include

inter	among
post	after
iuxta	near
versus	towards, against
per	by, through
apud	at, near, among
secundum	according to
ad	to, at

A few prepositions take either the ablative or the accusative according to their function. When they denote motion towards the accusative is used; when they denote rest, the ablative is used.

in	into, against, in, on
sub	up to, under
super	over, upon
subter	under

Exercise 14
Translate the following, accounting for the case, number and gender of the nouns, pronouns and adjectives (including those which follow prepositions)

(a) *Ego, Ricardus, ecclesie Sancti Leonardi totam terram cum pertinenciis confirmo*
(b) *Rex domino unam acram prati e terris dat*
(c) *Curia tenta* ('held') *die Lune proximo* ('next') *post festum Sancti Barnabe*
(d) *Curia tenta die Martis in festo Sancte Juliane*
(e) *Nicolaus Bond opponit se* ('appears in court') *versus Henricum et Aliciam*
(f) *Elena levat hutesium super Radulphum*

ADVERBS can modify a verb, an adjective or another adverb.

> She **unjustly** raised the hue and cry
> It was **unpleasantly** hot
> You performed **very** well

Adverbs are formed in a number of ways but except in their comparative and superlative forms (e.g. 'better', 'best', to be dealt with later) they do not change.

Exercise 15
Guess the meanings of these adverbs, then check

> *bene, libere, quiete, falso, optime, breviter, facile*

Exercise 16
Translate

(a) *Matilda iniuste levavit* ('raised') *hutesium*
(b) *Tenet tenementum libere et quiete imperpetuum*
(c) *Robertus solvit annuatim ijs. ad terminum Sancti Martini*
(d) *Johannes le Bonde cariat duas carectatas usque Bronston*
(e) *Henricus debet sarcliare* ('must hoe') *uno die* ('for one day') *sine cibo contra festum Sancti Petri*
(f) *Samuel Emery et Samuel filius suus tenent parcellam terre iuxta regiam viam*

You have now been introduced to well over 100 Latin words in exercises based upon extracts from actual local history documents. Let us revise the grammar. Most of the verbs used have been of the FIRST CONJUGATION although we have also met a few verbs e.g. *solvit, opponit, habet* (cited here in their third person, singular, present tense form) from other conjugations which will be dealt with later. Most of the nouns so far encountered have been of the FIRST DECLENSION but we have also met a few nouns of the SECOND DECLENSION. Latin nouns change their endings according to their function in the sentence and we have had many examples of the six case-endings, **nominative** (used for the subject of a sentence), **vocative** (exclamatory), **accusative** (used for a direct object and after certain prepositions), **genitive** (indicating possession and translated as 'of'), **dative** (used for the indirect object and generally translated by the word 'to' or 'for'), and **ablative** (used by itself to mean 'by, 'with' or 'from' and after some prepositions, for example 'in'). NOUNS may be singular in number or plural, and if there is a plural subject there will be a plural verb. ADJECTIVES must have the same case, number and gender as the nouns which they qualify. CONJUNCTIONS join words, phrases and clauses (sentences within longer sentences) and don't change, nor do PREPOSITIONS which show relationships between words. ADVERBS, which change only in their comparative and superlative forms, qualify a verb and often correspond to English adverbs ending in '-ly'.

Using the Glossary
(NOUNS)

In the glossary in this book (and in most dictionaries) nouns are shown in their nominative form, to save repetition and space the stem is shown by a hyphen followed by the letters which form the genitive ending, and the gender is also indicated, thus: *hercia, -e* (f.) 'harrow'. This means that the noun is of the feminine gender and the genitive case is *hercie*. The genitive ending is shown because by this ending you can generally recognise the declension to which the noun belongs—in this case the first declension, because it ends in *-e*. Another example of a noun is *campus, -i* (m.) 'field', which is masculine, has the genitive ending *-i* and therefore is of the second declension. Having established the declension to which the noun belongs by reference to the genitive you can then refer to the appropriate table in the appendices to this book for a model of the complete declension. Consulting the glossary on verbs will be dealt with later when we have seen tenses other than the present.

Chapter 2

Verbs of the Second Conjugation; Past and Future Tenses; Third Declension Nouns; Relative Pronouns; Adjectives which decline like Third Declension Nouns; Present, Past and Future Participles; the Ablative Absolute construction

Verbs of the SECOND CONJUGATION are characterised by an 'e' in the ending. Two verbs of this conjugation frequently met in local history documents are

Singular		**Plural**	
habeo	I have	*habemus*	we have
habes	thou hast	*habetis*	you have
habet	he/she/it has	*habent*	they have
teneo	I hold	*tenemus*	we hold
tenes	thou holdest	*tenetis*	you hold
tenet	he/she/it holds	*tenent*	they hold

Exercise 17
Guess the meaning of the following verbs from English words derived from them, check, then write out the full conjugation, present tense, of the first two. (Can you do this yet without looking at the models?)

video, iaceo, maneo, moveo, sedeo

Exercise 18
Translate

(a) *Una* (One) *acra in prato iacet*
(b) *Parsonam in ecclesia video*
(c) *Ecclesia tenet iij rodas in manerio*
(d) *Willelmus et Alicia uxor eius* ('his wife') *tria messuagia ad voluntatem* ('at the will') *domini tenent*

The INFINITIVE form of the verb has already been mentioned, as having the preposition 'to' in front of it. It signifies a general activity or state without any alteration of its ending to denote person, number or tense. Thus

laborare est orare 'to work is to pray'
contains two infinitives of the first conjugation.

The PAST TENSE of a verb is formed by adding an ending to a stem slightly changed from the stem of the present tense. Here is the past perfect tense of the verb *aro* ('to plough') which we have seen previously only in the present tense; stem is *arav-*

Singular		Plural	
arav-i	I have ploughed (or I ploughed)	*arav-imus*	we have ploughed
arav-isti	thou hast ploughed	*arav-istis*	you have ploughed
arav-it	he/she has ploughed	*arav-erunt*	they have ploughed

Exercise 19

Guess the meanings of any of the following verbs which are new to you, check, then write out the past perfect tense forms of the first two on the model of *aro* above (omitting the dash).

occupo, assigno, condono, presento, warantizo

Regular verbs of the second conjugation have a characteristic '-u-' in the stem of the perfect tense but the endings are the same as those of the first conjugation. Thus *teneo* 'to hold' has the perfect stem *tenu-* and conjugates thus:

Singular		Plural	
tenui	I have held (or I held)	*tenuimus*	we have held
tenuisti	thou hast held	*tenuistis*	you have held
tenuit	he/she/it has held	*tenuerunt*	they have held

Which translation you use—'he held' or 'he has held'—depends on the context. In deeds and charters normally use the latter form:

Sciant omnes quod ego Henricus de Daneston assignavi unum burgagium Ranulpho
Know all (men) that I, Henry of Daneston, have assigned one burgage to Ranulph

Exercise 20

Guess the meanings of any new words, check, then write out the past tense of the following regular second conjugation verbs: *moneo, habeo, debeo*

Exercise 21

Translate, explaining the case, number and gender of the nouns and adjectives

(a) *Quo die* ('On which day') *comparuit et dominus monuit eum* ('him')
(b) *Sewinus faber quattuor acras terre in manerio tenuit* ('held' is better here than 'has held')
(c) *Ego, Bertram de Verdun, pro anima mea* ('my') *et pro anima Rohais uxoris mee* ('of Rohais my wife') *totam terram de Croxden deo et beate Marie dedi* ('have given') *et hac* ('by this') *carta confirmavi*
(d) *Adam tannator debet apparentiam et non venit* ('has not come') *et curia amerciavit eum vj denarios pro defalta curie*

So far we have dealt only with regular verbs, that is, verbs whose tense-forms do not differ from those in the standard model. Some irregular verbs have non-standard stems. For example while *do* 'to give' as we have seen follows the usual pattern of a first conjugation verb in its present tense *do, das, dat, damus, datis, dant,* it has a different stem for the perfect tense, *ded-* to which standard endings are added:

	Singular		**Plural**
dedi	I gave (or have given)	*dedimus*	we gave
dedisti	thou gavest	*dedistis*	you gave
dedit	he/she gave	*dederunt*	they gave

Exercise 22
Translate explaining case, number and gender of the nouns and adjectives

(a) *Agricola terras suas* (his) *aravit*
(b) *Rex domino terram in parochia dedit*
(c) *Nos, Willelmus et Elizabetha, ix acras pasture Willelmo filio nostro confirmavimus*
(d) *Sciant omnes quod ego, Johannes, x rodas prati ecclesie Sancti Petri dedi et hac carta confirmavi*
(e) *Ricardus et Radulphus dederunt clameum quod habebant in pastura de Edulneston monachis de Tuttesbir imperpetuum*

If the verb is irregular, you will always find the stem given in the word list or dictionary. Thus

> *video* I see *videre* to see *vidi* I saw
> *visum* having (been) seen (this last stem is explained later)

In this verb the past perfect stem is irregular though the endings remain standard. The verb conjugates as follows in the perfect tense

	Singular		**Plural**
vidi	I saw (have seen)	*vidimus*	we saw (have seen)
vidisti	though sawest (hast seen)	*vidistis*	you saw (have seen)
vidit	he/she saw (has seen)	*viderunt*	they saw (have seen)

Exercise 23
Translate. (Henceforward you need not account for the case-endings unless you find, after checking your answers, that you have made a mistake. In this case determine for yourself whether it is just a slip or you have not yet assimilated a basic principle. If the latter, study the appropriate section again.)

(a) *Villani in crastino Sancti Martini campos araverunt*
(b) *In burgo predicto unum pratum habuimus*
(c) *Ego, Johannes de Halton, armiger, dedi et hac carta mea confirmavi Henrico filio Thome portarij illas* ('those') *terras quas* ('which') *in parco tenebam*
(d) *Willelmus filius Nicholai tenet unum messagium cum curtilagio et solvit elemosinario ijs. vjd*

We have seen how Latin verbs work: there is a basic stem, which changes for different tenses, and standard endings which denote person and number. So you can anticipate how the FUTURE TENSE, and indeed other tenses, are going to be formed. For example *warantizo* 'to warrant', a first conjugation verb much used in deeds of title, conjugates in the future as follows:

warantiza-bo	I will warrant (i.e. guarantee)
warantiza-bis	thou wilt warrant
warantiza-bit	he/she will warrant
warantiza-bimus	we will warrant
warantiza-bitis	you will warrant
warantiza-bunt	they will warrant

The characteristic endings of a regular future verb of the first and second conjugations are, as you see, *-bo, -bis, -bit, -bimus, -bitis, -bunt.*

The same principle applies to the IMPERFECT tense which corresponds to the English past continuous tense 'was -ing'

attachiabam	I was distraining, or I distrained
attachiabas	thou wert distraining
attachiabat	he was distraining
attachiabamus	we were distraining
attachiabatis	you were distraining
attachiabant	they were distraining

It will now be apparent to you that the ability to translate Latin readily depends on how quickly you can become familiar with the endings of the various tenses as well as the vocabulary. Do not worry that *pro tempore* you have to look up so much in the tables and glossary. You will speed up later.

Exercise 24
Translate

(a) *Et ego et heredes mei* ('my heirs') *predicto Willelmo predictum tenementum warantizabimus et acquietabimus imperpetuum*
(b) *Dominus ecclesie dedit prata que* ('which') *in parochia tenebat*
(c) *Monachi pro anima domini Radulphi orabunt*

THIRD DECLENSION nouns have various endings in the nominative singular case. Recognise this declension by its genitive form which ends in *-is* (not to be confused with dative and ablative plurals of the first and second declensions).

	Singular	Plural
Nom.	(various)	*-es*
Voc.	(various)	*-es*
Acc.	*-em*	*-es*
Gen.	*-is*	*-um* or *-ium*
Dat.	*-i*	*-ibus*
Abl.	*-e*	*-ibus*

Some nouns with a syllable more in the genitive singular than in nominative singular e.g. *pons, pontis* (m. 'bridge) have their genitive plural in *-ium*, so in this case it is *pontium*.

Ensure that in the third declension you add endings to the TRUE STEM, which you get from the genitive form given in the dictionary by leaving off the *-is*.

Here are two nouns of the third declension fully declined:

| | *rex* (m.) 'king' | | *heres* (m.,f.) 'heir' | |
	Singular	**Plural**	**Singular**	**Plural**
Nom.	*rex*	*reges*	*heres*	*heredes*
Voc.	*rex*	*reges*	*heres*	*heredes*
Acc.	*regem*	*reges*	*heredem*	*heredes*
Gen.	*regis*	*regum*	*heredis*	*heredum*
Dat.	*regi*	*regibus*	*heredi*	*heredibus*
Abl.	*rege*	*regibus*	*herede*	*heredibus*

true stem *reg-*   true stem *hered-*

The third declension contains nouns of all genders

Exercise 25
Guess the meanings of, check, and write out the full declension singular of the first two of these nouns

uxor, Trinitas, assumptio, abbas, donatio, salus

Neuter nouns of the third declension have the same forms for the nominative, vocative and accusative cases both singular and plural. (The third declension is complex with numerous exceptions from the models. Remember to find the TRUE STEM before you add endings.)

nomen (n.) 'name'

	Singular	**Plural**
Nom.	*nomen*	*nomina*
Voc.	*nomen*	*nomina*
Acc.	*nomen*	*nomina*
Gen.	*nominis*	*nominum*
Dat.	*nomini*	*nominibus*
Abl.	*nomine*	*nominibus*

Exercise 26
Guess the meanings of, check, and write out the full declension both singular and plural of the following third declension neuter nouns:

opus, corpus, jus (ius)

Using the Glossary: a step by step example.

Remember that you identify third declension nouns by the *-is* ending of the genitive case; endings are added to the true stem which is found by removing the *-is* from the genitive. Suppose the sentence to translate is

Johannes apparet in curia cum fratribus suis

We will also suppose you can already do the first part—'John appears in court'— but are uncertain about the remainder. In the glossary you find *frater*, *fratris* (m.) 'brother'. You know that this is a third declension noun by the ending of the genitive form, therefore you turn to the model of this declension in the appendix, where you find that the ending *-ibus* can be a dative plural meaning 'to' or 'for', or an ablative plural meaning 'by', 'with' or 'from'. In the glossary again you find that *cum* is a preposition, meaning 'with' and it is followed by a noun in the ablative case. Your translation reads so far 'with brothers' and you are left with *suis*, an adjective, which can be ablative plural of *suus* 'his'. It agrees therefore in gender, number and case with *fratribus* and so your translation must be

'John appears in court with his brothers'

You have proved to yourself that this answer is grammatically correct. Everything fits in Latin, if you persevere, as it does in a Roman mosaic.

RELATIVE PRONOUNS like 'who' or 'which' are used to connect sentences or clauses. Take the two sentences

The farmer ploughs the land. He holds the land

You can make these into one sentence by using the relative pronoun 'which':

The farmer ploughs the land which he holds

In Latin the relative pronoun changes its form for case, gender and number. The rule is that the relative pronoun takes its **number** and **gender** from its antecedent, that is the word in the first or main clause it refers to, but its **case** from its function in its own clause, that is, depending on whether it is the subject or object of the verb or has some other role. Thus in the sentence above the antecedent to 'which' is 'land'. 'Land' is the direct object of 'ploughs' and in Latin is therefore singular in number and feminine in gender.

Agricola arat terram	*Terram tenet*
The farmer ploughs the land	He holds the land

When these two sentences are joined we have

Agricola terram arat quam ('which') *tenet*
The farmer ploughs the land which he holds

and we have used a relative pronoun *quam* instead of repeating the word *terram*. The form *quam* is used because it is singular in number and feminine in gender to agree with its antecedent *terram* and is accusative in case because it is the direct object of 'holds'. It isn't the subject: 'He', the subject, is already contained in the verb *tenet*.

Now an example of the relative pronoun when it is the subject.

> The farmer ploughs the land which lies in the parish
>
> *Agricola terram arat que in parochia iacet*

Why *que*? Here the relative pronoun *que* is singular and feminine, like its antecedent *terram* but it the subject of the verb *iacet* ('lies') and therefore is nominative in case.

The various forms taken by the relative pronoun for different cases, genders and numbers are as follows:

	Singular				**Plural**			
	Masc.	Fem.	Neut.		Masc.	Fem.	Neut.	Meaning
Nom.	*qui*	*que*	*quod*		*qui*	*que*	*que*	'who' 'which'
Voc.	—	—	—		—	—	—	
Acc.	*quem*	*quam*	*quod*		*quos*	*quas*	*que*	'Whom' 'which'
Gen.	*cuius*	*cuius*	*cuius*		*quorum*	*quarum*	*quorum*	'whose'
Dat.	*cui*	*cui*	*cui*		*quibus*	*quibus*	*quibus*	'to whom'
Abl.	*quo*	*qua*	*quo*		*quibus*	*quibus*	*quibus*	'by whom'

Note there is no vocative form.

Exercise 27

Translate and explain the gender, number and case of the relative pronoun in the sentence below on the following model:

> *Video dominum qui cartam dat*
>
> I see the lord who gives the charter

qui is masculine and singular agreeing with its antecedent *dominum* and nominative because it is the subject of the verb *dat*.

(a) *Regina domino terras dat quas in Anglia habet*
(b) *Hoc* ('this') *est pratum quod multas vaccas habet*
(c) *Edwardus ecclesie prata dedit que in manerio tenebat*
(d) *Robertus agricola est cui terram do*
(e) *Rex dominis terras dedit quorum milites fortiter pugnaverunt*
(f) *Willelmus dominus est cuius terre in parochia iacent*
(g) *Ranulphus duas acras tenet quarum una acra iuxta terram Johannis iacet*
(h) *Ego Ranulphus comes do et hac carta confirmavi Waltero filio meo pratum quod habebam in parochia*
(i) *Hec* ('this') *est carta qua terram teneo*

ADJECTIVES in addition to declining like first and second declension nouns have a third declension form: the vowel in the ablative singular case-ending changes from -e to -i, the genitive plural can end in -ium and the accusative neuter plural ends in -ia. Like nouns adjectives of this declension are found with varied nominative forms:

finalis (m. and f.), *finale* (n.) 'final'; *acer* (m. and f.), *acre* (n.) 'sharp'

Here is one model, *omnis* 'all', a word much used in local history documents.

	Singular			Plural		
	Masc.	Fem.	Neut.	Masc.	Fem.	Neut.
Nom.	*omnis*	*omnis*	*omne*	*omnes*	*omnes*	*omnia*
Voc.	*omnis*	*omnis*	*omne*	*omnes*	*omnes*	*omnia*
Acc.	*omnis*	*omnis*	*omne*	*omnes*	*omnes*	*omnia*
Gen.	*omnis*	*omnis*	*omnis*	*omnium*	*omnium*	*omnium*
Dat.	*omni*	*omni*	*omni*	*omnibus*	*omnibus*	*omnibus*
Abl.	*omni*	*omni*	*omni*	*omnibus*	*omnibus*	*omnibus*

As you see many of the endings are the same.

Exercise 28

Translate, stating and accounting for the case, number and gender of the adjectives.

(a) *Ego Ricardus de Bronston dedi et hac* ('by this') *carta mea* ('my') *confirmavi Henrico de Winshill omnia messuagia que habebam in parochia*

(b) *Nos Johannes de Brailes et Agneta uxor mea confirmavimus Rogero capellano omnes meas terras cum omnibus pratis eisdem* ('to the same') *pertinentibus* ('belonging') *ad terminum vite sue* ('his')

(c) *Item lego Michaeli rectori ecclesie parochialis ijs.vjd.*

(d) *Predictus Johannes cepit de domino omnia et singula premissa predicta pro serviciis debitis* ('for services owed') *secundum consuetudinem manerij predicti*

(d) *Et dat domino de fine* ('for a fine') *ad ingressum suum* ('his') *xijd.*

PRESENT PARTICIPLES are partly adjectives and partly verbs. It follows that they must agree with the nouns they refer to in case, number and gender. There was an example, *pertinentibus*, in Exercise 28(b) above, where the participle agreed with *pratis* in being ablative, plural and neuter. Present participles derive from their verb and often correspond to the English ending '-ing'. Thus *pertinentibus* comes from *pertineo* 'to belong to'. To form the present participle add -ans to the stem of a first conjugation verb, -ens to the second and third and -iens to the fourth. Here is a model of the declension of a present participle deriving from a second conjugation verb much used in local history documents when specifying the location of a piece of land or tenement:

iacens 'lying'

	Singular		**Plural**	
	Masc/Fem	Neut.	Masc/Fem	Neut.
Nom.	*iacens*	*iacens*	*iacentes*	*iacentia*
Voc.	*iacens*	*iacens*	*iacentes*	*iacentia*
Acc.	*iacentem*	*iacens*	*iacentes*	*iacentia*
Gen.	*iacentis*	*iacentis*	*iacentium*	*iacentium*
Dat.	*iacenti*	*iacenti*	*iacentibus*	*iacentibus*
Abl.	*iacenti(e)*	*iacenti(e)*	*iacentibus*	*iacentibus*

Notice that except for nominative and vocative singular present participles have a -*t* in the stem. Notice also that the ablative singular ends in -*i* when it is used as an adjective; in the ablative absolute construction (to be explained later) it is always -*e*.

Ubi est terra iacens in manerio?

Where is the land lying in the manor?

iacens is nominative, because it agrees with *terra* which is the subject of the sentence even though it follows the verb, and also singular in number and feminine in gender.

Exercise 29
Translate, stating and accounting for the case, number and gender of the participle.

(a) *Ubi est via ducens ad villam?*
(b) *Video viam ducentem ad villam*
(c) *IX acre terre arabilis iacentes in villa predicta dimittuntur* ('are demised') *abbatie*
(d) *Nos Johannes de Hopton et Matilda uxor mea Gilbertum attornatum constituimus* ('have appointed') *dantes eidem plenam potestatem*
(e) *Henricus de Verdon dat abbatie de Croxden unam virgatam terre cum omnibus pratis iacentibus in manerio suo*

PAST AND FUTURE PARTICIPLES are much used in local history documents. They are formed from the last of the four key parts of a verb which are usually shown in a glossary or word list. Thus you will find

voco, -are, -avi, -atum 'to call'

To save space, for regular verbs, usually only the first word is shown in full and the stem of the verb, in the above case *voc-*, is represented by a dash for the other parts, thus

voco   means 'I call' (first person, sing., present tense)
-are   signifies 'to call' (the infinitive)
-avi   signifies 'I called' or 'have called' (first person, sing. perfect)
-atum (This is known as the supine base and from this base, *vocat-* the past and future participles (and some tenses in the PASSIVE VOICE—to be dealt with later) are formed.

To form the past participle change the final *-m* of the supine to *-s* thus, *vocatus*, and then decline it like a first or second declension adjective, making it agree with the noun it refers to.

dominus vocatus Henricus	the lord called Henry (nom., sing., masc.)
domina vocata Elizabetha	the lady called Elizabeth (nom., sing., fem.)
campum vocatum Oxhay	the field called Oxhay (acc., sing., masc.)
in terris vocatis Broadholme	in the lands called Broadholme (abl., plur., fem.)

and so on.

Classical Latin (except for deponent verbs) lacks an active past participle and thus *vocatus* strictly means 'to have been called' and not 'to have called', but medieval usage sanctions the simple translation 'called'.

Exercise 30

Translate, stating and accounting for the case, number and gender of the present and past participles

(a) *Regina dedit Willelmo terram vocatam Horsehay*
(b) *Messuagium vocatum Hautassise iacet in Bradeway*
(c) *Hac carta indentata virgatam terre Ranulpho confirmavimus*
(d) *Andreas Paschal, generosus, filius Andree Paschal, militis, tenet unum messuagium vocatum Foxholes*
(e) *Hec est finalis concordia facta in curia regis*
(f) *Franciscus Bartlett tenet unam acram pasture iacentem in campo iuxta venellam vocatam Le Hey*
(g) *Willelmus Normansell sursumreddit in manus domini duo clausa iacentia in parochia que tenuit iure Elizabethe uxoris sue*

The FUTURE PARTICIPLE is formed from the supine by changing the final *-m* of the stem of the verb to *-rus, -ra, -rum* which then declines like a first/second declension adjective *bonus -a -um*. It is mostly found in its nominative and dative plural forms at the beginning of deeds and charters.

> *Omnibus fidelibus Christi hoc scriptum visuris vel audituris*
> To all Christ's faithful who will see or hear this writing

visuris is the dative plural form of the future participle of *video, videre, vidi, visum* 'to see' (notice the irregularity in the change from *'d'* to *'s'*); it agrees with *fidelibus*. *audituris* is dative plural future particle of *audio, audire, audivi, auditum* 'to hear' (fourth conjugation see next chapter).

> *Noverint universi has litteras visuri vel audituri*
> Know all (men) about to see or hear this letter

visuri and *audituri* are nominative plural future participles agreeing with *universi*

Adopt this procedure in translating.

- find the main verb, and ensure you have translated the person, number and tense correctly
- look for the subject by asking 'Who or what is the sentence about?' remembering it will be in the nominative case, singular or plural, either expressed separately or already contained in the verb
- look for a direct object (if the verb is transitive) in the accusative case
- look for an indirect object (to whom something is given) in the dative case
- look for adjectives, present/past/future participles, in the same case, number and gender as the nouns to which they refer
- look for prepositions which connect nouns and check the cases by which they are followed
- analyse the case of each noun, asking yourself what is its case and why is it in that case?
- remember it is the endings of the words which are decisive and not the order in which they are found in a sentence

It is usually possible to prove to yourself that your translation is grammatically correct.

The Ablative Absolute Construction

This construction frequently consists of a noun or pronoun and a participle (or another noun or adjective) both in the ablative case. It is independent of the grammatical construction of the rest of the sentence (hence the term *absolutus* 'set free' from which it is derived), but it defines a circumstance connected with the action of the sentence or adds information.

The ablative absolute is often found in deeds as part of the *testimonium* or witnessing

Hiis testibus Roberto de Alton, Henrico de Rocester ...
These (being) witnesses Robert of Alton, Henry of Rocester

There is no present participle meaning 'being' in Latin and you have to 'understand' this without its being expressed, just as *est* 'is' may often be omitted.

concessi ecclesie totam terram excepto prato
I granted all the land, except the meadow, to the church

This is an example of an ablative absolute consisting of a noun and a past participle.

The ablative absolute can often be neatly translated as a subordinate clause dependent on 'When':

fidelitate facta Johannes admissus est tenens
When he had done fealty John was admitted tenant

Exercise 31
Translate

(a) *Nicolas Bold et Robertus Bydell decenarii presentant Thomam Clerke et Henricum Chatcull pro defectu apparantie*
(b) *Ricardus Messing obstupavit viam ducentem ad ecclesiam*
(c) *Ad hanc curiam venit Johannes Welles armiger et sursumreddit in manus domini unum cotagium nuper in tenura Roberti Turner*
(d) *Dedit ecclesie unum tenementum abbuttans borealiter super viam vocatam Le Flete*
(e) *Edwardus Aston miles tenuit de domino per copiam rotuli duo prata iacentia inter terras Johannis Wise et viam regiam*
(f) *Juratores elegunt* ('elect') *in officio decennarii Johannem Sale.* ('He is') *Juratus*
(g) *Idem Radulphus nativus levabit fenum unum diem per annum*
(h) *Franciplegii presentant quod* ('that') *Isabella que fuit* ('was') *uxor Thome de Rideware et que debet apparentiam* (i.e. in court) *non venit ideo ipsa* ('she') *in misericordia* (*est*, 'is', omitted but understood and should be added to translation)
(i) *Noverint universi* ('Know all men') *presens scriptum visuri vel audituri quod ego Henricus priori et monachis de Tutbury duo cotagia cum pertinenciis iacentia in villa predicta dedi et hac carta mea confirmavi*
(j) *Johannes Bardell tenet certas parcellas terrarum dominicalium et reddit per annum xiijs. iiijd.*
(k) *Prestito juramento dominus absolvit eam*

Chapter 3

Third and Fourth Conjugation Verbs; the Infinitive; the Accusative and Infinitive Construction; the Subjunctive Mood; the Passive Voice; Gerunds and Gerundives; Pronouns; Irregular, Deponent and Impersonal Verbs; Comparison of Adjectives and Adverbs

So far we have used mostly verbs of the first and second conjugations. The third conjugation is slightly more complex, with its present stem ending in a consonant or -*u*.

Singular		**Plural**	
dico	'I say'	*dicimus*	'we say'
dicis	'thou sayest'	*dicitis*	'you say'
dicit	'he/she says'	*dicunt*	'they say'

Notice the -*i* in the endings except for the first person singular and third person plural.

Exercise 32
Translate

(a) *Juratores dicunt quod omnia bene* ('All is well')
(b) *Ricardus remittit totum ius suum*
(c) *Edward Aston diem clausit extremum* ('has died', literally 'has closed his last day') *et accidit domino taurus*
(d) *Precipimus pro nobis et heredibus nostris quod predicta villa sit liber burgus* ('may be', subjunctive)
(e) *Dominus predictus concedit burgo gildam mercatoriam*

Third conjugation verbs do not have the -*b*- element of a first or second conjugation verb (e.g. *confirmabo* ('I shall confirm') in the FUTURE tense: the predominant vowel is -*e*-

Singular		**Plural**	
concedam	I shall grant	*concedemus*	we will grant
concedes	thou wilt grant	*concedetis*	you will grant
concedet	he will grant	*concedent*	they will grant

The IMPERFECT tense of a third conjugation verb has endings similar to those of the first and second conjugations

pascebam, pascebas, pascebat, pascebamus, pascebatis, pascebant
'to pasture/feed' (i.e. cattle)

29

Exercise 33

Guess the meanings of, and write out the full conjugation in the present, future and imperfect tenses of

claudo, tango, mitto

Verbs of the fourth conjugation have a present stem ending in *-i* but are otherwise similar in form to verbs of the third conjugation.

audio 'I hear' (stem audi- add standard endings)

Present	Future	Imperfect
audio	audiam	audiebam
audis	audies	audiebas
audit	audiet	audiebat
audimus	audiemus	audiebamus
auditis	audietis	audiebatis
audiunt	audient	audiebant

Exercise 34

Translate

(a) *Et super hoc venit predictus Johannes in eadem curiam et cepit de domino predicta crofta tenenda sibi et heredibus suis*

(b) *Et nos, predictus Henricus et predicta Margareta warantizabimus acquietabimus et defendemus illas terras contra omnes gentes*

(c) *Scient omnes* ('Know all men') *quod nos Henricus de Denstone et Margareta uxor mea dedimus Willelmo Welles omnes terras quas tenebamus in manerio de Alton*

The stems of the PERFECT TENSE of third conjugation verbs are formed in a variety of ways and cannot be determined from the present stem: you must consult the glossary. The endings, however, are the same as for the first and second conjugations. Here are some of the ways in which perfect stems are formed

with -xi   dico, dicere, dixi, dictum ('I say/speak')

	Singular		Plural
dixi	I said/have said	diximus	we said/have said
dixisti	thou saidst/has said	dixistis	you said/have said
dixit	he/she said/has said	dixerunt	they said/have said

with *-si*   e.g. *clausi*   from *claudo, claudere, clausi, clausum* 'to close/enclose'

with reduplication of a consonant e.g. reddidi from
reddo, reddere, reddidi, redditum 'to pay/return'

There are numerous other forms and many irregularities e.g. *capio* 'I take' changes its vowel in the perfect tense and conjugates

cepi, cepisti, cepit, cepimus, cepistis, ceperunt

Using the Glossary and Tables

Suppose you have the sentence

Johannes Brown deposuit quod Henricus debet vj solidos

and you do not immediately recognise the verb *deposuit*. Look in the word list or dictionary for words beginning with *depo-* and you will find *depono, deponere, deposui, depositum* (3), 'to depose or state'. The table with the model of a third conjugation shows the ending *-it* is the third person, singular of the perfect tense. The translation must be

'John Brown deposed (stated) that Henry owes 6 shillings.

Exercise 35
Translate

(a) *Dominus accepit terras*
(b) *Ego Ricardus remisi totum ius meum*
(c) *Nos Willelmus et Elizabetha apposuimus nostra sigilla*
(d) *Valentinus bis braciavit*
(e) *Robertus dabit domino xijd*
(f) *Samuel Lathropp admissus est tenens* ('was admitted tenant') *et fecit domino fidelitatem*
(g) *Ricardus Porter diem clausit extremum citra ultimam curiam*
(h) *Juratores elegerunt Johannem Blount decennarium pro anno*
(i) *Dictus Radulphus solvet domino annuatim ij solidos*
(j) *Adam le Verdon dimisit tradidit et concessit Radulpho de Hassal unum burgagium, cum edificiis in villa de Ruthin*

The FUTURE PERFECT tense is used in Latin in a logical if, in modern English usage, slightly pedantic way.

English: I shall give you the book when I have finished it
Latin: I shall give you the book when I shall have finished it

Such a construction is often found at the beginning of medieval charters and deeds.

Omnibus Christi fidelibus ad quos presentes lettere pervenerint
To all Christ's faithful to whom the present letters shall (have) come

To form the future perfect tense 'shall have ...' add *-ero, -eris, -erit, -erimus, -eritis, -erint* to the perfect stem.

Look up *pervenio* in the word list and you find

pervenio, pervenire, perveni, perventum

'to come to, arrive at'

So you see the perfect stem to be *perven-* to which the appropriate endings must be added.

The INFINITIVE as seen earlier is that form of the verb which in English is preceded by the preposition 'to' and expresses a generalised action which is not limited by person or number. In Latin there are three active voice infinitive forms (the active and passive voices are explained later)

> present active infinitive formed by adding *-are, -ere, -ere, -ire* to the present stem of a first, second, third or fourth conjugation verb e.g. *confirmare* 'to confirm', *tenere* 'to hold', *claudere* 'to close', *venire* 'to come'

> perfect active infinitive formed by adding *-isse* to the perfect stem e.g. *confirmavisse* 'to have confirmed' (when the stem ends in *-v*, a shortened form may often be found in which the *-vi* is omitted e.g. *confirmasse*)

> future perfect active infinitive formed by changing the *-m* of the supine base to *-rus*, and adding *esse* (the present infinitive of the verb 'to be' e.g. *confirmaturus esse* 'to be about to confirm'

The Infinitive is often found in medieval deeds in what is known as the ACCUSATIVE AND INFINITIVE construction

Sciant omnes me Ricardum confirmare cartam

(Literally) 'Know all (men) me Richard to confirm the charter'
but to be translated, 'Know all men that I, Richard, confirm the charter'

The past infinitive is more usual in this construction

Sciant omnes me Ricardum confirmavisse cartam
Know all men that I, Richard, have confirmed the charter

You can see from these examples why the construction is called accusative and infinitive:

omnes	is the subject in the nominative case
Sciant	is the verb
me Ricardum	are the direct objects of the verb and therefore in the accusative case, and are followed by an infinitive, either present or perfect.

Sometimes the medieval scribe used an anglicised construction with no accusative case and no infinitive

Sciant omnes quod ego, Ricardus, confirmavi cartam
Know all men that I Richard have confirmed the charter
(the translation is exactly the same)

Exercise 36
Translate

(a) *Sciant omnes me Willelmum dedisse Elene, filie mee, unum messuagium*
(b) *Sciant qui sunt et qui futuri sunt* ('present and future men') *me Stephanum concessisse unam hidam terre Deo et Sancte Marie*
(c) *Notum sit* ('Be it known') *nos Johannes de Bronston et Elizabetha uxor mea confirmavisse Humberto unam acram terre arabilis iacentem in manerio de Tatenhill et abbuttantem super communem viam*

In Exercise 33(c) above there is a new form of verb *sit*, a third person singular present tense in the SUBJUNCTIVE MOOD. The Latin verb in addition to tenses has three MOODS which require different endings to be added to the stem. So far in this book the verbs used have been mainly in the INDICATIVE mood when the activity is real—'I am king'—there is no doubt about it. The subjunctive is the mood of doubt, hypothesis or unreality—'If I were king'—(but I'm not!), 'May the queen live for ever' (but she won't!). Note almost the last trace of the subjunctive left in English in the use of 'were' after 'if'—'If I were you' (not 'If I was you' which still grates badly). In Latin the subjunctive mood would be used. The third mood is the IMPERATIVE in which there is a command or order e.g. 'Beware of the dog' (in Latin *Cave canem*) but this is not often found in local history research. The subjunctive in local history Latin lacks the refinements of classical Latin, but look for four main usages, each of which, as you see from the examples, has an element of uncertainty about it

• as a main verb of a sentence at the beginning of deeds and charters, as above in Ex.34(c)

Sciant omnes ...
'Let (i.e. May) all men know ...'

• again as a main verb, giving an order (which is not put into the imperative mood)

Preceptum est quod Henricus distringatur
It is ordered that Henry should be distrained
(subjunctive in passive voice, see later)

• to express a condition

Si contingat ... If it should happen

• after the preposition *ut* with verbs of entreating, commanding, persuading, effecting etc.

ut hec carta remaneat imperpetuum
in order that this charter may remain (i.e. in force) for ever

The subjunctive is found in various other constructions and situations but the uses above are those most commonly encountered. The occasions when it is employed are fairly regular and in practice you will have no difficulty in translation.

Using the Glossary for the Subjunctive

Suppose you didn't know *Sciant* above. Looking in the glossary for verbs beginning with *Sc-* you find *scio, scire, scivi, scitum* (4). It is a fourth conjugation verb so look at the model, *audio* in the tables of conjugations; there is only one similar ending *audiant* so your verb must be the same, third person, plural, present and subjunctive. It remains to find the most appropriate English translation.

There are four tenses of the subjunctive, present, imperfect, perfect and pluperfect. All are shown by models in the tables at the end of the book. Below are only the present tenses of the four conjugations for the two moods

	Present Indicative		**Present Subjunctive**	
1st Conj.	rogo	'I ask'	rogem	Observe the change of
	rogas		roges	vowel from -a- to -e-
	rogat		roget	in the ending
	rogamus		rogemus	
	rogatis		rogetis	
	rogant		rogent	
2nd Conj.	teneo	'I hold'	teneam	
	tenes		teneas	
	tenet		teneat	Note the addition of
	tenemus		teneamus	-a- in the subjunctive
	tenetis		teneatis	ending
	tenent		teneant	
3rd Conj.	peto	'I petition'	petam	
	petis		petas	
	petit		petat	The characteristic -i-
	petimus		petamus	in the indicative
	petitis		petatis	ending becomes -a- in
	petunt		petant	subjunctive
4th Conj.	scio	'I know'	sciam	
	scis		scias	
	scit		sciat	again the subjunctive
	scimus		sciamus	ending adds an -a-
	scitis		sciatis	
	sciunt		sciant	

No specific translation of verbs in this mood can be given because it depends on the clause or way in which the verb is used. Such words as 'let', 'may', 'might', 'should', 'be', etc. can be appropriate. There is no future tense in the subjunctive mood.

Exercise 37
Translate

(a) *Si teneat domos solvat redditum*
(b) *Preceptum est distringere Henricum et quod sit ad proximam curiam*
(c) *Requiescat in pace*
(d) *Notum sit universis audituris vel visuris has litteras*
(e) *Et ordinatum est quod nullus tenentiarius permittet ullum alium tenentiarium secum cohabitare in domo* (the scribe uses an ordinary future here)
(f) *Pateat universis quod ego, Robertus, constitui Gilbertum attornatum meum*
(g) *Si contingat quod dicta Elizabetha obierit sine heredibus legitimis predicte terre remaneant Johanni*

The ACTIVE VOICE expresses what the subject of a verb is or does: *valeo* 'I am well', *dominus confirmat cartam* 'the lord confirms the charter'

The PASSIVE VOICE expresses what is done to the subject, e.g. *carta confirmatur a domino* 'the charter is confirmed by the lord', *carta civibus datur* 'a charter is given to the citizens'.

Here are the endings of the present tense active and passive voices of a first conjugation verb side by side for contrast

	Active			Passive	
condon-o	'I excuse'		*condono-r*	'I am excused'	
condona-s	'thou excusest'		*condona-ris*	'thou art excused'	
condona-t	etc.		*condona-tur*	etc.	
condona-mus			*condona-mur*		
condona-tis			*condona-mini*		
condona-nt			*condona-ntur*		

Refer to the tables at the end of the book for the forms taken in both the active and passive voices of all the tenses in all four conjugations. The passive voice endings are similar for all four conjugations. There are passive subjunctive forms as well. Do not try to remember all the endings but learn how to consult the tables quickly to speed up your translation.

Exercise 38
Translate

(a) *Omnes terre in manu domini capiuntur*
(b) *Franciplegii presentant Adam obstupavit viam communem et preceptum est ballivo quod distringatur*
(c) *Margareta in misericordia pro transgressione per aucas suas in prato domini sed quia pauper misericordia remittitur* (The verb *est* is omitted twice in this extract)
(d) *Placitum inter Johannem Wryght et Simonem de Hanbur ponitur in respectu ad proximam curiam*

The passive voice is found in all tenses, e.g. in the first conjugation the third person singular is

carta datur	the charter is given	(present)
carta dabatur	the charter was being given	(imperfect)
carta dabitur	the charter will be given	(future)
carta data est	the charter has been/was given	(perfect)
carta data erat	the charter had been given	(pluperfect)
carta data erit	the charter will have been given	(future perfect)

A perfect tense in the passive voice as seen above consists of a past participle, e.g. 'given', 'confirmed', plus a part of the irregular verb 'to be' (*sum, fui, esse, futurus*) and it is necessary first to conjugate this verb because it is used as an auxiliary to form tenses of other verbs.

Present		**Imperfect**		**Future**	
sum	'I am'	*eram*	'I was'	*ero*	'I will be'
es	'thou art'	*eras*	'thou wert'	*eris*	'thou wilt be'
est	'he/she/it is'	*erat*	'he/she/it was'	*erit*	'he/she/it will be'
sumus	'we are'	*eramus*	'we were'	*erimus*	'we will be'
estis	'you are'	*eratis*	'you were'	*eritis*	'you will be'
sunt	'they are'	*erant*	'they were'	*erunt*	'they will be'

The past participle, the first element in the perfect passive verb, agrees with the noun it refers to in case, number and gender, declining like the adjective *bonus, bona, bonum* ('good').

To form the perfect passive put together the past participle in its correct form and the appropriate part of the verb 'to be'.

carta data est

'the charter was (has been) given'

Here *data* is nominative, singular, feminine, agreeing with *carta*

dominus vocatus est Henricus

'the lord was called Henry'

Here *vocatus* is nominative, singular, masculine agreeing with *dominus*

villani attachiati sunt

'the villeins were attached'
(i.e. their goods were distrained to ensure appearance at court)

Here *attachiati* is nominative, plural masculine agreeing with *villani*

Using the Glossary

To form the past participle passive of a verb, change the final *-m* of the supine base to *-s* and, as stated above, decline like *bonus -a -um*

Here is an example of a first conjugation past participle passive

voco, vocare, vocavi, vocatum 'to call'

	masc.		fem.		neu.	
	Sing.	Plur.	Sing.	Plur.	Sing.	Plur.
Nom.	*vocatus*	*vocati*	*vocata*	*vocate*	*vocatum*	*vocata*
Voc.	*vocate*	*vocati*	*vocata*	*vocate*	*vocatum*	*vocata*
Acc.	*vocatum*	*vocatos*	*vocatam*	*vocatas*	*vocatum*	*vocata*
Gen.	*vocati*	*vocatorum*	*vocate*	*vocatarum*	*vocati*	*vocatorum*
Dat.	*vocato*	*vocatis*	*vocate*	*vocatis*	*vocato*	*vocatis*
Abl.	*vocato*	*vocatis*	*vocata*	*vocatis*	*vocato*	*vocatis*

There is no past participle active in Latin: *vocatus*, in classical Latin would be translated 'having been called', not 'called' and medieval usage often tolerates the greater use of the past participle as an adjective. The past perfect tense is sometimes formed not with *sum, es, est* etc. but with *eram, eras, erat* etc.

Edwardus baptisatus est, Edwardus baptisatus erat
both can mean the same—'Edward was baptised'.

Exercise 39

Translate

(a) *Messuagium vocatum est Highlands*
(b) *Magistri licenciati sunt*
(c) *Galfridus et Radulphus admissi sunt tenentes*
(d) *Elizabetha filia Johannis Port baptisata erat*
(d) *Croftum tentum est per servicia inde debita et consueta*
(e) *Item lego Margarete filie mee et heredibus eius de proprio corpore legitime procreatis duo burgagia*

The PASSIVE INFINITIVE has three tenses in classical Latin but the future passive infinitive is not usually found in local history documents so is here omitted. Compare the two voices in each tense of a first conjugation verb:

(Present)	Active	*obligare*	'to bind'	
	Passive	*obligari*	'to be bound' (change final *-e* to *-i*)	
(Perfect)	Active	*obligavisse*	'to have bound'	
	Passive	*obligatus esse*	'to have been bound'	

2nd conj.	*teneri*	'to be held'	*tentus esse*	'to have been held'
3rd conj.	*regi*	'to be ruled'	*rectus esse*	'to have been ruled'
4th conj.	*audiri*	'to be heard'	*auditus esse*	'to have been heard'

In practice you will find little difficulty with the passive infinitive but you need to recognise the form especially as it appears regularly in marriage bonds in the accusative and infinitive construction.

Noverint universi me, Johannem Moore, teneri et firmiter obligari ...
Know all men that I, John Moore, am bound and firmly held ...

(See also next chapter)

Gerunds and Gerundives

The gerund is a verbal noun, that is, it has some of the features and functions of both a verb and a noun: it acts like a verb and it declines like a neuter singular noun of the second declension. It is often the equivalent of the English noun ending in '-ing' but can equally often be translated by a simple infinitive. It is formed by adding a standard ending, *-ndum* or *-endum* to the present stem of the verb, and is then declined on the following model:

	1st Conj.	2nd Conj.	3rd Conj.	4th Conj.
Nom.	—	—	—	—
Acc.	*levandum*	*habendum*	*solvendum*	*veniendum*
Gen.	*levandi*	*habendi*	*solvendi*	*veniendi*
Dat.	*levando*	*habendo*	*solvendo*	*veniendo*
Abl.	*levando*	*habendo*	*solvendo*	*veniendo*
	'raising'	'having'	'paying'	'coming'

Note there is no nominative form.

The gerund is much used in medieval documents

after the preposition *ad* to express purpose:
ad levandum redditus 'to collect the rents': here the gerund is accusative and is followed by its own direct object *redditus*

both by itself and after the prepositions *de, in, pro* etc. the ablative gerund is used:

tenet messuagium faciendo servicia debita et consueta
'he holds a messuage by doing the services owed and accustomed'

Here the gerund *faciendo* is in the ablative and is followed by an accusative plural neuter direct object *servicia*

The GERUNDIVE can sometimes be difficult to distinguish from the gerund and in the abbreviated Latin of local history documents it may not be certain what construction the scribe had in mind. It may indeed not always make a difference to the translation. The gerundive is a passive verbal adjective, not a verbal noun like the gerund, deriving from a verb but used mainly as a sort of adjective. It is formed by changing the final *-m* of the gerund into *-s* and is then declined to agree in case, number and gender with the noun to which it refers.

> *... confirmavi predictum croftum habendum et tenendum Alicie*

(Literally)
'... I have confirmed the aforesaid croft to be had and to be held to Alice'

(Rendered into legal English)
'... I have confirmed the aforesaid croft to have and to hold to Alice'
(i.e. to be held by Alice, but the dative case is used in this construction and should be so translated)

habendum and *tenendum* are here accusative singular neuter gerundives in agreement with *croftum* (although they look like accusative gerunds)

Both the gerund and gerundive usually contain the idea that something should be done or is to be done and the translation includes such phrases as 'to be paid'. The constructions are often found in deeds of gift and financial transactions recorded in manorial court rolls (see Chapters 5 and 6 also).

Exercise 40
Translate

(a) *dedi ecclesiam habendam et tenendam Phillipo pro octo solidis michi annuatim reddendis*
    (there are three gerundives here)
(b) *Predicta Katerina concessit Johanni patri suo anum messuagium tenendum ad totam vitam suam*
(c) *Ego Radulphus obligatus sum Humberto Pole in decem libris bone et legalis monete Anglie*
(d) *Et dat ad ingressum v solidos solvendos ad festum Purificationis*
(e) *Consideratum est quod dicti Nicholaus et Johannes habeant diem concordandi*
    (a genitive gerund but to be translated 'for ...'; explain also the form of *habeant*)

PRONOUNS stand in place of a noun. There are numerous classes of pronouns and some also serve as adjectives. Like nouns, pronouns take case-endings.

Personal pronouns are 'I', 'you', 'he' etc.

	Singular				**Plural**			
	1st Person		**2nd Person**		**1st Person**		**2nd Person**	
Nom.	*ego*	I	*tu*	thou	*nos*	we	*vos*	you
Acc.	*me*	me	*te*	thee	*nos*	us	*vos*	you
Gen.	*mei*	of me	*tui*	of thee	*nostri*	of us	*vestri*	of you
Dat.	*michi*	to me	*tibi*	to thee	*nobis*	to us	*vobis*	to you
Abl.	*me*	from/ by me	*te*	from/ by thee	*nobis*	from/ by us	*vobis*	from/ by you

nostri and *vestri* are in some constructions *nostrum* and *vestrum*

michi is the medieval form of *mihi* 'to me'

For the personal pronouns of the 3rd person, use the demonstrative pronouns

is, ea, id

Singular

	Masc.		**Fem.**		**Neut.**	
Nom.	*is*	he	*ea*	she	*id*	it
Acc.	*eum*	him	*eam*	her	*id*	it
Gen.	*eius*	his	*eius*	hers	*eius*	its
Dat.	*ei*	to him	*ei*	to her	*ei*	to it
Abl.	*eo*	from/by him	*ea*	from/by her	*eo*	from/by it

Plural

	Masc.		**Fem.**		**Neut.**	
Nom.	*ei*	they	*eae*	they	*ea*	they
Acc.	*eos*	them	*eas*	them	*ea*	them
Gen.	*eorum*	theirs	*earum*	theirs	*eis*	theirs
Dat.	*eis*	to them	*eis*	to them	*eis*	to them
Abl.	*eis*	from/by them	*eis*	from/by them	*eis*	from/by them

The dative and ablative plurals are sometimes found as *iis*

There are more pronouns which can also be used as adjectives

	Pronoun	Adjective
hic, hec, hoc	he, she, it	this
ille, illa, illud	he, she, it	that
ipse, ipsa, ipsum	he, she, it (-self)	the same
idem, eadem, idem	he, she, it	himself, herself, itself

meus, tuus, suus 'my', 'thy', 'his' are Possessive Pronouns only used as adjectives

Exercise 41

Translate and explain the grammar of the pronouns and adjectives in the following phrases

hoc scripto meo;
dans eidem plenam potestatem;
hac mea carta indentura;
ad hanc curiam;
in illo messuagio;
Elizabeth et Galfridus et Henricus filius eorum;
dixit super sacramentum suum;
cum omnibus pertinenciis eisdem spectantibus ('belonging');
hec est finalis concordia

Irregular Verbs

Irregular verbs are those which are formed from more than one stem or root and whose tenses differ in form from those of regular conjugations. We have seen already *do, dare, dedi, datum* a first conjugation verb with an irregular perfect stem. Another very important verb is *possum* 'I can' or 'I am able' whose stem is *pot-* sometimes changing to *pos-*. The present tense conjugates as follows:

Singular		**Plural**	
possum	I can	*possumus*	we can
potes	thou canst	*potestis*	you can
potest	he can	*possunt*	they can

DEPONENT VERBS are partly passive in form but active in meaning. e.g. *sequor* has the *-or* ending of a passive voice but means 'I follow' not 'I am followed'. There are quite a few deponent verbs encountered in local history research, e.g. *conqueror* 'I complain'. There are also a few SEMI-DEPONENT verbs in which only the perfect tense and those tenses based on it are of passive form but active meaning, e.g. *soleo, -ere, solitus sum* (2) 'to be accustomed'.

Exercise 42
Translate

(a) *Edwardus non potest aliquod* ('any') *titulum in prato exigere* ('demand')
(b) *Robertus et heredes sui non possunt aliquod ius clamare*
(c) *Adam Hichen conqueritur de Henrico Bust de placito debito* (Despite the passive ending of the 3rd third person singular, *-tur* it is Adam who is complaining that Henry owes him money)
(d) *Nicholas le Comber queritur de Johanne de Stapenhill de placito transgressionis*
(e) *Divina officia laudibiliter observantur*
(f) *Galfridus de Monte calumpniatur* (passive not deponent) *quia destruxit herbagium vicinorum cum averiis suis*
(g) *Margareta de Lacy summonita fuit ad respondendum Alicie uxori Johannis Broun de placito defamationis* (Explain the grammar of *summonita* and *respondendum* in this extract taken from a manor court roll. We were not told what Margaret actually called Alice!)

IMPERSONAL VERBS as the term implies can only have 'It' as a subject. Compare English 'It is raining'. They exist in all tenses but are usually only found in the present and perfect tense. Some impersonal verbs are followed by a dative of the person/s concerned, some by an accusative and some by a genitive.

Exercise 43
Translate

(a) *Pateat universis per presentes* (i.e. writings or letters)
    (Here is an impersonal verb also in the subjunctive mood)
(b) *Licet eis hoc facere*

(c)   *Oportuit eum venire*
(d)   *Compertum est per homagium quod Willelmus Michell obijt citra ultimam curiam*
(e)   *Preceptum est ballio seisire optimum animal ipsius Willelmi pro herietto*
(f)   *Notum sit universis ...*

ADVERBS show how, when or where the action of a verb takes place and as the word implies they add something to the verb.

Tenent terras quiete et libere
They hold the lands quietly and freely

Most adverbs are derived from adjectives. They are formed in two main ways: add *-e* to the stem of the adjective; thus *lat-us* 'wide' becomes *late-e* 'widely'. But a few adverbs so derived take an *-o* after the stem e.g. *falsus* 'false' becomes *falso* 'falsely'.
Add *-iter* to the stem; thus *laudabil-is* 'praiseworthy' becomes *laudabil-iter* 'laudably'.
Some adverbs are irregular e.g. *bonus* 'good' *bene* 'well'. Some adverbs are not based on adjectives e.g. *nunc* 'now', *semper* 'always', *non* 'not'.

Comparison of Adjectives and Adverbs

Adjectives, dealt with earlier only in their positive form, also have comparative and superlative forms. The comparative is formed by adding *-ior* to the stem and the superlative by adding *-issimus*

durus 'hard'; durior 'harder'; durissimus 'hardest'

The comparative adjective declines like a third declension noun but with a nominative singular in *-ior* and *-ius*

Positive: *tristis, -e*: 'sad' (stem *tristi-*).
Comparative: *tristior*, 'sadder'.
Superlative: *tristissimus*, 'saddest'.

Singular

	M.F.	M.F. & N.	N.
N.V.	*tristior*		*tristius*
Acc.	*tristiorem*		*tristius*
Gen.		*tristioris*	
Dat.		*tristiori*	
Abl.		*tristiore*	

Plural

	M.F.	M.F. & N.	N.
N.V.	*tristiores*		*tristiora*
Acc.	*tristiores*		*tristiora*
Gen.		*tristiorum*	
Dat.		*tristioribus*	
Abl.		*tristioribus*	

	Singular		
	M.	**F.**	**N.**
N.V.	*tristissimus*	*tristissima*	*tristissimum*
Acc.	*tristissimum*	*tristissimam*	*tristissimum*
Gen.	*tristissimi*	*tristissime*	*tristissimo*
Dat.	*tristissimo*	*tristissime*	*tristissimo*
Abl.	*tristissimo*	*tristissima*	*tristissimo*

	Plural		
	M.	**F.**	**N.**
N.V.	*tristissimi*	*tristissime*	*tristissima*
Acc.	*tristissimos*	*tristissimas*	*tristissima*
Gen.	*tristissimorum*	*tristissimarum*	*tristissimorum*
Dat.	*tristissimis*	*tristissimis*	*tristissimis*
Abl.	*tristissimis*	*tristissimis*	*tristissimis*

Adverbs do not decline but they do have comparative and superlative forms. To form the comparative adverb add -*ius* to the stem, and to form the superlative adverb add -*issime* to the stem.

late 'widely' *latius* 'more widely' *latissime* 'most widely'

There are a few irregular formations but the local historian is unlikely to encounter these.

Exercise 44
Translate

(a) *Licet Henrico illas terras occupare sine redditu*
(b) *Cum* (When) *diem clauserit extremum dominus percipiet melius averium*
(c) *Ad faciendum solucionem obligo me et heredes meos* (gerund followed by direct object)
(d) *Walterus dei gratia episcopus Lichfeldensis dilectissimo filio in Christo magistro Roberto archidiacono suo salutem*
(e) *Ideo ipsi remanent in misericordia prout patet super eorum capita* (i.e. the amount of the fine has been written above their names)
(f) *Petunt diem veredicto dicendo* ('for a verdict to be declared') *et eis conceditur.* (Explain the grammar of *dicendo*)
(g) *Johannes Payne cognovit se tenere libere per cartam unum messuagium*

We have now covered enough Latin grammar for you to be able to translate a variety of types of local history document. Although many additions and exceptions to the general rules have necessarily been omitted you will be able now to cope with most of the Latin in those sorts of document you are likely to encounter in your research. Do not expect yet to be able to read at sight: you will constantly need to use the glossary and tables of conjugations and declension. If you have forgotten or not yet fully assimilated a point, use the index of grammatical terms to refer back to the text. By reaching this point you have shown that you have mastered the basic principles of the language and can now attempt to apply your skills to the translation of actual documents. The remainder of this book offers help with understanding their structure and vocabulary.

Part 2
THE USES OF LATIN

Chapter 4

Ecclesiastical Records: Parish Registers, Marriage Licences and Bonds, Episcopal Visitations and Church Court Records, Early Sepulchral Inscriptions, Wills

Parish Registers

The Latin of parish registers is usually minimal, although sometimes the incumbent may have used Latin to make notes or comments. Early parish registers, from Thomas Cromwell's mandate of 1538, were kept in Latin but the practice was beginning to fade out by the first decade of the 17th century, went out completely during the Commonwealth period and resumed only here and there after 1660. Very few parish registers were recorded in Latin after the 1731 Act came into force, although this statute strictly applied only to civil and not to ecclesiastical records. Bishops' Transcripts, copies of the parish registers sent yearly to the bishop, are usually in the same language as the originals. Many parish registers have been transcribed and translated (and often published by parish register societies) but they can contain mistakes and omit entries and it is always useful, and sometimes necessary, to check with the originals.

The basic Latin vocabulary commonly used in parish registers consists of only 50 to 60 words, summarised below for convenience but also appearing in the Glossary. The opportunity is taken to revise a few grammatical points.

Baptismal Entries

baptisatus -a est -erat -fuit	was baptised (nom., sing., m. and f.)
baptisati sunt -erant -fuerunt	were baptised (nom., plur., m.)
baptisati, baptismata	the baptised
renatus -a -i	reborn (i.e. in baptism)
gemelli, gemini	twins
nomina baptisatorum	the names of the baptised (plur. of neuter *nomen* + genitive plur.)
baptizarium	payment to priest

Illegitimacy

Numerous nouns, adjectives and expressions denoting illegitimacy testify to the concern of the parishioners over a possible burden on the rates.

bastardus -a,
spurius -a, } illegitimate
illegitimus -a,
nothus -a, gnotus -a

ignoti parentis of unknown parents (gen. sing. *parens, -tis*)

filius -a {
adulterinus -a
terre
meretricis (gen. sing. *meretrix* f. 'harlot')
vulgi ('of the people')
populi ('of the people')
scorte (gen. sing. *scorta* f. prostitute)
}

natus -a ex fornicatione (abl. after preposition *ex*)

Marriages

nomina nuptorum the names of the married (neut. and gen. plur.)

nupti erant
conjuncti fuerunt
mariti fuere (shortened form)   were married, were joined in matrimony,
connubio juncti erant   contracted matrimony
copulati sunt in matrimonio
contraxerunt matrimonium

nuptiae solemnitizatae the marriage was solemnised (NB classical ending *-ae* sometimes used in parish registers)

uxorem duxit he took to wife (3 decl. acc. f., and 3rd pers. perf. of *duco*)

Burials

nomina defunctorum	the names of the dead
nomina sepultorum	the names of the buried
sepultus -a	buried
aborsus	miscarriage (*aborsus, -us,* m.)
mortuus -a	dead
vidua -e	widow

Other Terms

adolescens	young man
caelebs, coelebs	single, unmarried
vagus -a / *peregrinus -a*	tramp, vagrant
economus, gardianus	churchwarden

Dates

Dates are usually expressed by an ablative case for both the ordinal number and the word 'day' and the genitive case of the word 'month' and of the name of the month, e.g.

sexto die mensis Januarii

On the sixth day of the month of January

The names of the months are adjectives agreeing with *mensis* (m.) month, and the three chief days of the Roman calendar (*Kalendae, Nonae, Idus*, all f.). *Aprilis* is declined like *tristis; September, October, November, December* have the nom. masc. sing. in -er, the rest like *bonus*.

Exercise 45
Translate

(a) *Janeta Barne filia Gulielmi Barne curati de Chester primo die mensis Martii baptisata fuit anno predicto*
   (account for the grammatical form of *curati*)
(b) *Henrici fil. Robertus sepultus*
   (Do not fall into the trap: look at the endings! Extend the abbreviation *fil.* to its full length)
(c) *Agneta fa. meretricis vocatae Aliciae baptisata septimo die Julii 1590* (Extend *fa.*)
(d) *Georgius Lee uxorem duxit Miriam Shemmonds decimo quarto die Novembris 1644*
(e) *Matrimonium inter Willelmum Gilbert et Elizabetham Marshall solemnizatum xv^{to} Octobris*
(f) *Johannes Elison die Dominica 4to Augusti dum oves pascit in campis, per militem percussus et vulneratus in cerebro ex quo vulnere ad sextum diem languebat et tunc mortem obiit et septimo die eiusdem mensis sepultus est et eodem die miles predictus suspensus est.* (An entry in the margin of a parish register of the Civil War period. One would have expected *pascebat* an imperfect tense).

Marriage Licences and Bonds
Among useful sources for genealogical information to be found in diocesan records are marriage licences and bonds. Most marriages were celebrated by the local minister after the calling of the banns, but a bishop, archdeacon or their surrogate, or one of the archbishops, could issue a licence on the basis of a sworn statement (allegation or affidavit) to the effect that there was no known impediment to the marriage. The prospective bridegroom and a relative or friend also had to be bonded in a sum of money that the statement was true. The use of the marriage allegation was abolished in 1823 but until 1837 marriages without banns could only lawfully be celebrated by a licence. The existence of marriage licences, bonds and allegations is not proof that a marriage actually took place.

Exercise 46
(a) *Fiat licencia inter Henricum Aldridge de civitate Lichfield, caeleben, 23 annos et ultra natum, et Mariam Parker parochie Aston super Trent in comitatu Derbiae solutam 25 annos natam*
   Fiat is 3 pers. sing. pres. subj. of command Coming from *fio, fieri, factus sum* 'to be made' and is translated 'Let there be (granted)'; the subject of this sentence is *licencia; caeleben* is in apposition to *Henricum*, and *solutam* ('single') to *Mariam*.
(b) *Fiat licencia inter Robertum Smith, solutum, 24 annos natum, de parochia Barton subter Needwood, et Annam Homfreys, solutam, 22 annos natam, de eadem parochia*

The first part of a marriage bond is often in Latin. The person making the bond acknowledges that he is held and firmly bound in a stated amount of money to be paid to an ecclesiastical official. The second part of the bond, the 'Condition of this Obligation', usually in English, states that, if there is no impediment to the marriage, the bond will not come into effect.

The first few lines of a marriage bond are as follows

Noverint universi per presentes me Johannem Moore de Bromley Abbatis in comitatu Staffordie yeoman teneri et firmiter obligari Reverendo in Christo Ricardo Raines Legum Doctori in centum libris bone et legalis monete Anglie solvendis Ricardo ...

Noverint is a perfect subjunctive of command, from *nosco, noscere, novi, notum,* whose present and future tenses mean 'to get to know' and whose perfect tense means 'to have got to know'; *universi* is the subject of the sentence. Translate simply as 'Let all (men) know' or 'Know all (men)'.

me Johannem is the first part of an accusative and infinitive construction; remember to turn it around into good English.

teneri and *obligari* are passive infinitives, part of the accusative and infinitive construction

libris ablative plural following *in*

legalis adjective in the genitive case agreeing with 'money'

solvendis is a gerundive in the ablative plural agreeing with *libris* and with the idea of obligation, translated 'to be paid'

The Latin part of the bond continues that the person who takes out the bond binds himself and his heirs to make the payment faithfully, and the bond is then dated and sealed.

... ad quarum quidem solucionem bene et fideliter faciendum obligo me et heredes, executores et Administratores meos. Sigillo meo sigillatum datum 25 die mensis Februarii anno domino 1720

solucionem 'payment' is the accusative object of the gerund *faciendum* which depends on *ad* and means 'to do'; *bene* and *fideliter* are adverbs qualifying the gerund.

Exercise 47
Translate

Noverint universi per presentes nos Robertum Vernon de parochia de Hanbury et Thomam Vernon yeoman teneri et firmiter obligari Reverendo in Christo Patri et Domino Ricardo permissione divina Episcopo Lichfieldensis in sexaginta libris bone et legalis monete Magne Britannie solvendis eidem Domino Episcopo

aut suo certo Attornato Executoribus vel Administratoribus suis ad quam
solucionem bene et fideliter faciendum obligo nos et Heredes nostros per presentes.
Sigillis nostris sigillatum datum 13 die mensis Octobris anno regni Domini
nostri Georgii dei gratia Magne Britanie Francie et Hibernie Regis fidei
defensoris etc. septimo Annoque Domini 1720

(Note that in the regnal year, in this instance 7 George 1, the word *anno* and the
ordinal number are normally separated by the royal title; *que* added to a word is simply
translated 'and').

Other types of bond, tuition, curation and administration are also found in diocesan
records.

In the medieval period marriage was preceded by espousal, which could be entered
into at the age of seven. Entries of espousals in parish registers are very occasionally
found.

Sponsalia inter Rogerum Burn et Elizabetham Poynton in debita iuris forma
transacta 10 die Martii 1634

Espousal between Roger Burn and Elizabeth Poynton was transacted in due
form of law 10 day of March 1634

(*debita* is an adjective in the ablative, *transacta* is the perfect passive participle
agreeing with nominative neuter plural *sponsalia*)

Episcopal Visitations and Church Court Records

Records of episcopal visitations and of the proceedings of church courts are found
from early medieval times, and form an important and bulky part of diocesan archives.
They are often written in an execrable hand but the Latin, although highly abbreviated,
is usually simple in construction. They contain much material useful for local historical
and genealogical research. The following exercises represent only a few of the sorts of
information which may be obtained. (Readers will profit from consulting A. Tarver
Church Court Records (Phillimore, 1994).)

A bishop or his official delegate was supposed to conduct a primary or first
visitation of his diocese in his initial year of office and then one every three or four
years. Laymen, usually the churchwardens of each parish, brought their 'presentments'
to the visitation centre, of which there was one for every three or four rural deaneries.
The following exercises provide a few examples of the kinds of information to be
obtained.

Exercise 48

Translate

(a) *Ranulphus Hardinge legit preces in capella de Thursfield sine licencia et docet*
    pueros in capella predicta
(b) *Ricardus Copland et Johanna eius uxor non cohabitant et dominus monuit eum ad*
    cohabitandum cum uxore alioquin ad freqentandum domum ad minus semel
    hebdomaditim sub pena ...

(c) *Ricardus Hassall et Anna Heath* (were presented) *pro adulterio. Quo die comparuit et fassus est crimen obiectum* (the accusation made). *Unde dominus iniunxit ei penitencias die solis in duas septimanas*
(*fassus est* is a deponent verb from *fateor* 'to confess')

(d) *Uxor Roberti Betson non frequentat ecclesiam. Citetur de novo* (anew). (*Citetur* is passive subjunctive)

(e) *Dominus iniunxit ei purgationem cum 4° manu vicinorum 4° Septembris proximo*
(The meaning is that he must clear himself by the compurgation of four neigh-bours i.e. their swearing to the truth of his statements and/or to his character)

(f) *Comparuerunt et dominus monuit eos ad reparandum pavimentum ecclesie citra festum omnium sanctorum proximum*

(g) *Deinde super humilitationem dominus iniunxit ei penitencias die solis promixo post lectionem 2ᵃᵉ lecturae*
(On his repentance presumably he had to stand publicly in the church in a white sheet following the reading of the second lesson. Note the classical *-ae*)

Before the dissolution of the monasteries a bishop had the right and duty to visit most Benedictine houses. Visitations on the eve of the dissolution can to some extent test the validity of the charges made by Henry VIII's commissioners against the monks in their *Compendium Compertorum* ('Book of Findings') and in the much quoted preamble to the 1536 Act that the religious in the lesser monasteries engaged in 'manifest sin, vicious, carnal and abominable living'. Starting with the head of the religious community each inmate was questioned separately by the bishop's visitor.

Exercise 49
Translate these extracts from a visitation to a Staffordshire abbey in 1524.

(a) *Dominus Willelmus Beane, abbas ... dicit quod monasterium liberum est omni ere alieno. Divina officia silentium et religionis essentialia laudabiliter observantur. Accessus suspectus mulierum prohibetur ad confratres et contra. Omnia alia bono ordine constituta sunt*
ere alieno ablative of *aes alienum* (n.) debt; *Divina officia* i.e. religious services or *Opus Dei*, the constant round of prayer which was the kernel of the monastic life; *Accessus suspectus:* some contact between monks and women was inevitable for monastic business

(b) *Frater Robertus Busby, prior, pietanciarius et camerarius ... seculares in choro tem-pore divinorum cantantes incedunt absque superpellicis ... Fratres non utuntur braccis. Frater Elkyn seminator est discordie et conciliorum revelator.*

(c) *Frater Thomas Baker ... Potus conventualis nimis tenuis est ...*

(d) *Frater Willelmus Edys, coquinarius non adest*

Early Sepulchral Inscriptions
While the Latin of inscriptions on sepulchral monuments of the 17th century and later is often difficult and written in heavy style with flowery adulatory phrases about the deceased this is not true of the Latin of medieval inscriptions. Here the difficulties that the local history student is likely to encounter are the lettering (Lombardic and black

letter), the problems of extending the abbreviations and the erasures of words and letters due to the ravages of time and man. The language of 13th- and 14th-century inscriptions is often Norman French, thereafter English and Latin, the latter presenting few problems grammatically. The vocative case, addressing God, Christ and passers-by, and the imperative mood, are often found. In the transcription of a 16th-century inscription which follows the extensions are placed within brackets.

> *Orate pro a(n)i(m)a d(omi)ni Joh(ann)is Gylbert olim socij istius collegij qui obiit xvj die men(si)s Julij A(nn)° d(omi)ni m(illesim)° CCCCCxiiij cuius a(n)i(me) propicietur deus ame(n)*

Pray for the soul of the master John Gylbert fellow of this college who died on 16th day of the month of July in the year of our Lord 1514 on whose soul may God have mercy

orate is a plural imperative 'pray ye'
anima is ablative after *pro*
socij is genitive of *socius*
istius is genitive of *iste* (declined like *ille*)
propicietur from *propicior* (sometimes found as *propitior*)

a deponent verb, literally 'to be propitious to', in the present subjunctive (because it expresses a wish which may not be fulfilled) and used with a dative.

Exercise 50
Translate

(a) *Fili dei miserere mei*
   Fili is an irregular vocative; *misereor* 'to pity' is a deponent verb, hence its passive form, which is followed by a genitive case; here the verb is in the imperative mood
(b) *Miserere mei et salve me quia speraui* (i.e. *speravi*) *in te*
   (The -*u* and -*v* are interchangeable)
(c) *Orate pro anima domini Radulphi quondam rectoris istius ecclesie*
(d) *Xpc dilexit nos et lauit nos a peccatis nostris in sanguine suo*
   xpc is an abbreviation for 'Christ' from the practice of reproducing in Latin texts the contracted form of the Greek word
(e) *Hic jacet Thomas ... qui quidem Thomas obiit ...*
   'which Thomas' but can be translated simply 'who died'
(f) *Hic jacent corpora Ludovici Bagot militis et Anne uxoris eius qui obiit quinto die Septembris ... quorum animabus propiciet Deus Amen*
   The date of Anne's death is not given
(g) *Anime vere dei gratia in pace quiescant*
   Anime is the nominative plural subject of the subjunctive *quiescant*

Abbreviations are part of the study of palaeography. Here are a few you may encounter:

Abbreviation	Extension	Meaning
a' a͞m͞e	amen	amen
ar' arm'	armiger	esquire
ai͞a	anima	soul
ai͞ab̄s	animabus	(for/to) the souls
at͞e	anime	to the soul
cu'	cum	with
cui'	cuius	of whom
De'	Deus	God
d͞m, d͞n͞s	dominus	lord, master, sir
ei'	eius	his, her
epi' ep͞s	episcopus	bishop
eccl͞e	ecclesie	of the church
fr'	frater	brother
gen'	generosus	gentleman
H S I	hic sepultus iacet	here lies buried
ihs	Jesus	
isti'	istius	of this
jac'	jacet	lies
m m°	mille millesimo	1000, in the 1000th year
mr	magister	master
m͞esis	mensis	month
M P	moerens posuit	he/she sorrowfully place
ob'	obiit	he/she died
p̄	per (+ accusative)	by, through
p̄	pro (+ ablative)	for
p̄pciet'	propicietur	may have mercy
q'	qui	who
quo' d͞a	quondam	formerly
quor'	quorum	whose
R I P	requiescat in pace	may he rest in peace
s'c'i	sancti	of Saint
u͞r ux	uxor	wife
XPC	Christus	Christ

Exercise 51

Translate this commonly found inscription. It is an exercise in the understanding of the various tenses and forms of the verb *sum, esse, fui* 'to be' and of the use of verbs in the imperative mood.

> *Quisquis eris qui transieris,*
> *Sta, perlege, plora;*
> *Sum quod eris, fueram quod es*
> *Pro me, precor, ora*

Precor is a deponent verb, present tense singular; note the use of the future perfect tense in the first line; if you can follow the grammar of this inscription you have made good progress.

Wills

Wills are a principal source of information to local and family historians. They are nearly all written in English from the mid-16th century when statutes of 1529 and 1540 regulated the procedures required to prove them. Earlier wills in Latin are in general confined to wealthier or titled people and most often were proved in the courts of York or Canterbury.

The content of wills naturally varies but standard expressions in the format usually include

- a heading *In nomine Dei amen* 'In the name of God, amen'
  a date expressed in relation to a saint's day and a regnal year of year of grace e.g. *in festo Sancte Anne anno domini millesimo cccc lvj*^{mo} 'in the feast of Saint Anne A.D.1456'
- the leaving of the testator's soul to God *lego animam meam Deo* 'I leave my soul to God'
- the naming of executors of the will *Ordino AB, CD, meos veros executors* 'I appoint AB CD my true executors'
- the citing of witnesses to the will *Hiis presentibus ...* 'these being present ...'
- the sealing of the will *In cuius rei testimonium huic testamento sigillum meum apposui* 'In witness of which to this testament I have affixed my seal'
- the date, if not already given, in which case you may find *Datum die et anno supradictis* 'Dated on the day and year above-mentioned'

Other expressions include *condo testamentum meum* 'I make my will', *volo quod* 'I desire that' following by a verb in the subjunctive, and *lego* 'I leave' or 'I bequeath' followed by an accusative direct object and a dative of the person to whom the bequest is made.

Exercise 52

Translate the following, all extracts from the same will but separated for convenience

(a) *In dei nomine amen die Jovis in festo Sancte Petronille virginis anno domini millesimo CCCC lxxxvij*^{mo} *Ego domina Alicia Lee condo testamentum in hunc modum In primis lego animam meam Deo patri omnipotenti Beate Marie ac omnibus sanctis corpusque meum ad sepeliendum ad placitum executorum meorum*
Note the gerund *ad sepeliendum* literally 'for burying' i.e. 'to be buried'

(b) *Item lego fratribus predicatoribus Novi Castri x s. ad celebrandum unum trentale Sancti Gregorii pro me et marito meo*
'Preaching Brothers' (i.e. Dominican Friars in this case); note another gerund; *trentale* 'an office of thirty masses'

(c) *Item volo quod executores mei solvant vel solvi faciant omnia debita que debeo*
The instruction to pay debts is often in the form of an absolute ablative *debitis meis prius solutis* 'my debts having previously been paid'

(d) *Item ordino et facio Hugonem Egerton et Radulphum Delves armigeros meos veros executores ut ipsi disponant omnia bona ac debita mea non legata ad honorem dei et utilitatem anime mee*
Note *disponant* 'may dispose of', a verb in the subjunctive mood in a subordinate clause introduced by *ut* 'in order that'

(e) *In cuius rei testimonium ego Johannes Soldus vicarius de Awdley huic presenti testamento sigillum meum apposui*
Why the vicar rather than the testator herself affixed his seal is not apparent.

A will is usually accompanied by the probate act which gave the executors permission to carry out the provisions of the will

Exercise 53
Translate with the aid of the grammatical and other notes

> *Probatum fuit suprascriptum testamentum coram domino apud Lambeth penultimo die mensis Novembris anno domini supradicto juramento Willelmi Wadham procuratoris et commissa fuit administracio Radulpho de Leye executori de bene et fideliter administrando citra festum purificationem beate Marie virginis proximo*

The subject is *testamentum* (n.); the will was proved in the Prerogative Court of Canterbury; *administracio* is the subject of the past perfect verb *commissa fuit* which agrees in case and gender with the subject; *administrando* is a gerund after *de*; the will was dated Thursday in the feast of Saint Petronilla, i.e. 31 May 1487, probate was granted on 29 November 1487 and the executors had until the feast of the Purification, 2 February 1488 to carry out the provisions of the will.

The probate of a will required the executors to furnish an inventory of the goods and chattels of the deceased. The inventory itself is usually in English but the grant of administration at the foot of the inventory is in Latin and can furnish extra genealogical detail.

Exercise 54
Translate

(a) *Fiat Administracio bonorum que fuerunt Johannis Allen nuper dum vixit parochie Cheadull, defuncti, Elizabethe Allen, vidue, uxori dicti defuncti.*
fuerunt 'which belonged to' or simply 'of'
(b) *Jurata dicta Elizabetha Allen coram me Thoma Hubbocke, deputato*
The grant was made to the widow who was sworn to carry out the provisions of the will
(c) *Obligantur Willelmus Harvey de Hulme in Comitatu Staffordie et Elizabetha Allen de Cheadle predicta*
Obligantur present passive plural 'are bound'

Chapter 5

The Records of the Manor

Except for the Commonwealth period, until the early 18th century manorial records were normally in Latin.

Manor Court Rolls

Court rolls, i.e. the records of the court held by the lord of the manor, reflect the varied functions of the manor, which was an economic unit in which all the tenants were bound to the lord, his free tenants, *liberi*, paying him rent, his unfree tenants, *villani*, doing weekly and seasonal labour service on the demesne (later commuted into money payments). All tenants regularly attended, as an obligation, the lord's local manor court for the settlement of their quarrels, the regulation of their communal agrarian affairs and the approval and registration of transfers of copyhold land. The amount of information, of a local historical, topographical, genealogical and demographic nature that can be derived or may be deduced from a lengthy series of court rolls, makes this type of document essential for research.

The record of a manor court opens with a heading giving the title of the court, sometimes the name of the lord, the date expressed in relation to a saint's day and regnal year and later the name of the lord's steward before whom (*coram* followed by ablative) the court was usually held. There are two main types of court, the court baron, usually held every three weeks, and the court leet, or view of frankpledge, held every six months.

Exercise 55

Translate

(a) *Curia baronis tenta apud Barton die Jovis proximo post festum Sancti Barnabe apostoli anno regni Henrici octavi dei gratia Anglie, Francie et Hibernie regis xxvij°*
Medieval Latin uses the past participle passive, in this extract *tenta*, loosely; translate as 'held'. To modernise dates it is necessary to refer to the appropriate book listed in the appendix or to other sources which provide tables of saints' days, regnal years and an Easter Day calendar. The modern form of the date above is given in the answer. *regis* is third declension genitive, in apposition to *Henrici*. Remember that the ordinal number of the regnal year, in Roman numerals or occasionally as a word, is usually separated from the word *anno* by the royal title.

(b) *Curia baronis apud Alrewas tenta in crastino Sancti Bartholomey anno regni regis Henrici filii regis Johannis xliij°*

(c) *Curia visus franciplegii tenta ibidem pro manerio predicto decimo die Octobris anno regni domine nostre Anne octavo*
This is the six-monthly court, the 'view', *visus* (fourth declension, genitive in -*us*)

After the heading come *Essonia* i.e. excuses for non-attendance presented by a proxy. Only three consecutive essoins were allowed (and noted) before the defaulter

57

owing 'common suit of court' was fined. Fines for non-attendance were a useful source of income to the lord. In a view of frankpledge the essoins are often followed by a list of sworn jurors who present the names of person who should have attended and have not done so.

Exercise 56
Translate

(a) *Robertus pistor essoniavit se* ('himself') *per Ricardum clericum de communi secta jᵒ*
(b) *Willelmus Adam essoniavit se per Hugonem messorem de eodem* ('of the same' i.e. suit of court) *ijᵒ*
(c) *Willelmus Docerill essoniavit se de apparentia per Willelmum Crocket jᵒ*
(d) *Juratores super sacramentum suum presentant quod persone sequentes debent sectam ad hanc curiam et fecerunt defaltam*

Then follow the presentments by frankpledges or tithingmen from each village in the manor of persons who had committed some offence. Brewing 'contrary to the assize' i.e. officially infringing the local regulations on price and quality, but in fact probably a form of unofficial licensing, was a frequent presentment. Assaults, especially serious where blood was drawn, are also common.

Exercise 57
Translate

(a) *Willelmus Wryght et Henricus frater eius traxerunt sanguinem de Hugone filio Walteri*
(b) *Franciplegii presentant quod Alana uxor Roberti Cuge vendidit servisiam contra assisam*
(c) *Franciplegius de Branston presentat quod Henricus le Cartwright braciavit contra assisam*
If the court decided that the person accused of an offence was guilty then the words 'he is in mercy' were usually added to the charge. This did not mean that the lord was going to exercise mercy but that a fine *amerciamentum* (n.) was to be imposed. The financial penalties imposed by the court are usually found inserted above the offender's name, not as an afterthought but because *afferatores* ('assessors') fixed the amount of the fine at the end of the court proceedings.
ijd.
(d) *Item presentant quod Ricardus Porter fecit affraiam super Johannem Cartwright contra pacem. Ideo ipse in misericordia* (*est* is usually omitted because it is understood to be there)
vijd.   vjd.
(e) *Xij juratores presentant quod Hugo de Menill et Robertus filius eius extraxerunt iniuste sanguinem de Roberto de Gresley qui attachiati fuerunt et invenerunt Johannem de Bursincot et Johannem de Stapenhill plegios ideo etc.*
Note the passive perfect tense *attachiati fuerunt*. Offenders had to find pledges i.e. sureties for the payment of any fine that was imposed. Here *plegios* is accusative plural in apposition to the two 'Johns'. The sentence 'Therefore he/she is' or 'they are' is often contracted to *Ideo etc.*

The manor court dealt with disputes concerning trespass, debt, etc. which had been brought before it. The plaintiff (*querens*) brought pledges for prosecuting his case (*ad prosequendum*) and the defendant (*defendens*) likewise for replying to the charge (*ad respondendum*). Sometimes they wagered their law (*vadio legem*) i.e. brought compurgators to vouch for the truth of their statements.

Exercise 58
Translate

(a) *Johannes Kemster queritur de Agnete de Ragleye de placito transgressionis*
(b) *Willemus Charle querens versus Robertum Laster de placito debiti. Plegii de prosequendo Johannes Hobbeson et Adam frater eius*
(c) *Inquisitio inter familiam Henrici de Fold et Aliciam uxorem Willelmi Orme de hutesio levato ponitur in respectu usque sabbato proximo*
   Manor courts were often slow in action. This was one in which the consideration of a dispute over the raising of a hue-and-cry was postponed.
(d) *Ricardus Rond opponit se* (literally 'offered himself' i.e. appeared in court) *versus Henricum de Wylinton qui non venit et plegius fecit defaltam ideo melius districtus [est].*
   If the litigant or a pledge failed to turn up he was summoned to appear again under a more severe penalty.

When such local disputes had been dealt with the court heard of any transactions concerning land within the manor. Copyhold tenure was the descendant of villein tenure; over the course of time labour services owed by the villeins on the manor had been commuted to a money rent, but copyhold tenants were required to make special payments to the lord of the manor when the tenement changed hands, and the change of occupancy had to be recorded in the manor court rolls. The language in which these transactions is recorded is standard 'common form'.

Exercise 59
Translate

(a) *Ad hanc curiam venit Johannes Bowyer et sursum reddidit in manus domini manerii predicti duas acras terre arabilis*
   Johannes the subject, follows the verb; it is impossible to tell from the form of *venit* whether it is either a present or a perfect tense; let the context decide and be guided by the scribe's precedents; there is no doubt however about the tense of *reddidit*, where the perfect stem is formed by reduplication *reddo, -ere, -didi, -ditum*
(b) *Ad hanc curiam venit Johannes Welles, armiger, et sursum reddidit in manus domini manerii unum cotagium et unum clausum ibidem pertinens nuper in tenura Roberti Turner defuncti*
   Explain the grammatical form of *pertinens* and *tenura* after you have done the translation.
   The court roll often records that the former tenant has surrendered the tenement to the 'use and behoof'—(*ad opus et usum*) of a named person and his heirs and assigns. The incoming tenant petitions to be admitted, and pays a fine at his entry. The transfer of the tenement was one some manors recorded in the rolls as *per virgam* 'by

the rod', a relic of the early livery of seisin, the ceremony by which possession of a tenement by a new tenant was symbolised by the handing over of a stick or piece of turf, etc. The new tenant then did fealty, *fecit fidelitatem* i.e. made an oath of allegiance, to the lord. In later times whether such ceremonies were fully carried out is uncertain but they continued to be recorded in many court rolls.

Now follows an actual extract in full from a manor court roll, the only simplification being that the abbreviations have been extended. If you can cope you have nothing to fear from the Latin of such copyhold entries in court rolls.

Exercise 60
Translate

> *Ad hanc curiam venit Henricus Shipton de Longdon in propria persona sua et in plena curia ille sursum reddidit in manibus domini manerii predicti per virgam secundum consuetudinem manerii predicti unam Rodam terre arabilis (sive plus sive minus) iacentem in Le Churchfield que Roda terre est pars cuiusdam messuagii prefati henrici Shipton ad opus et usum Willelmi Pott heredum et assignatorum suorum imperpetuum. Et super hoc in istam curiam venit Willelmus Pott et petivit admitti tenens et dedit domino pro fine ad ingressum tres solidos et fecit fidelitatem et admissus est inde tenens*

Translate *ille* simply as 'he'; note that the tenement is surrendered into the hands (plural) of the lord; *que* is adjectival 'which rod'; *prefati* is often used instead of *predicti; petivit admitti tenens* 'he petitioned to be admitted tenant'; the meaning is clear even if the grammar is complex: *admitti* is a passive infinitive, and in this construction it is prolative, i.e. it carries on the meaning of the previous verb *petivit*—what did he petition for? *admitti* is also a copulative verb, that is, it links the subject 'he' with a complement 'tenant' which is in the same case, nominative, as the subject; this construction is frequently encountered and you should know the grammatical explanation; *inde* is susceptible of a number of translations: 'thence' or 'thereupon' will do.

Manor court records of transactions concerning land held on servile tenure can be useful clues to local demographic history when they show that the change of tenant has been caused by death. In the medieval period many people lived close to the edge of starvation and a series of bad harvests or the outbreak of plague could result in a sharp increase in local mortality. This is to some extent reflected in the number of deaths of villein tenants recorded in the manor court rolls.

The next exercise is taken from the court rolls of a rural manor in Staffordshire at the time of the Black Death.

Exercise 61
Translate

(a) *Curia tenta die Sabbati ante festum Nativitatis Johannis Baptiste anno regni regis Edwardi tercij post conquestum vicesimo tercio* (20 June 1349)
(b) *Thomas de Curbeye qui tenuit de domino j messuagium et unam virgatam terre decessus (est) et dominus habet pro herrieto j bovem pretii ij solidos*

The heir of a deceased tenant paid a heriot, usually the 'best beast' but commuted to a money payment to the lord in order to come into his inheritance; *decessus* is third person singular perfect passive; the medieval scribe abbreviated the Latin word for 'price', *pretium* (n.) to *p't* which is here extended into the genitive form though an ablative is also possible.

(c) *Thomas Gyn qui tenuit de domino j messuagium et dimidiam virgatam terre decessus [est] et dominus habet j juvencam pretii xvij denarios*

(d) *Thomas le Creighton qui tenuit j messuagium decessus et dominus habet pro herietto j vaccam pretii xviij d.*

Rentals

Manorial records may include rentals, i.e. lists of tenants, their holdings and the rents they paid. Urban rentals often give street names and provide other local place-names. A rental was sometimes made and renewed—*factum et renovatum*—on the oath of local inhabitants.

Here are a few extracts from an abbey rental of 1319. The abbot was lord of the manor, which had evolved into a sizeable borough, so many of the tenements were burgage plots paying a money rent.

Exercise 62

Translate

(a) *Galfridus de Kingston tenet j burgagium quondam Alani cirotecarii solvendo abbati xijd*
  quondam should be translated as 'formerly belonging to' followed by a name in the genitive case; *solvendo* is an ablative gerund from *solvo* to pay; strictly to be translated 'by paying' but 'paying' will do.

(b) *Elena filia Walteri tinctoris tenet pratum vocatum Skyrmere quondam patris eius et extendit se usque pontem novum solvendo elemosinario iij s*
  'stretching as far as'; the rent of this tenement has been earmarked for the almoner's department of the abbey

(c) *Incipit Newestrete*
  Robertus de Winshull tenet j burgagium super quod habet ij messuagia quondam Willelmi de Palmer de Wynshull solvendo sacriste xij d

(d) *Memorandum quod istud burgagium fuit quondam Ricardi Quenyld carpenterii filii Rogeri nativi qui duxit Agnetam Bronemay que fuit filia Ricardi del Fold qui quidem Ricardus factus est postea leprosus et recessit ad domum leprosorum sine herede ...*
  The scribe noted these complex and slightly ambiguous genealogical details because of their possible financial significance; the tenement had descended from a villein, there was no heir because the last occupant suffered from leprosy and therefore the tenement might escheat back into the hands of the abbot; *duxit* stands for *uxorem duxit*

(e) *Johannes filius Johannis de Cloddeshale tenet iij burgagia quorum ij fuerunt quondam Ricardi le Webbe pro escambio unius acre in Cuccnonmedwe pro quibus nihil solvit racione escambio et solvit pro tercio abbati xij d*
  Note the ablative case after *'pro'* and the genitive *unius* but smooth out the translation to 'in exchange for one acre in Cuckoomeadow'.

Now a few extracts from a rental of an estate owned by a secular lord of the manor in the later 16th century.

Exercise 63

Translate

(a) *Rentale factum et renovatum per sacrum Johannis Blounte et Arturi Meverell xx^{mo} Aprilis anno regni domine nostre Elizabethe xv^{to}*

(b) *Johannes de London tenet unum cotagium et unam acram terre que reddere solebat per annum iijs.vjd. modo ijs*
    soleo 'to be accustomed' is one of a class of verbs known as semi-deponents in which only the perfect and the tenses based upon it are of passive form but active in meaning; here the meaning is clear—'which used to pay'.

(c) *Redditus unius messuagii dimissi heredibus Edwardi Proudeholme ad voluntatem domini reddendum inde per annum ixs.iiijd*

(d) *Thomas Hyron et Johannes Alporte tenent certas parcellas terrarum dominicalium et reddunt per annum xiijs.iiijd.*
    Notice the two different genitive plural endings, one in *-rum* and the other in *-ium*

Custumals

A custumal is a survey of rents and customary obligations owed by tenants to the lord of the manor. They are found from the 12th century to the later 14th century when the increasing substitution of rents for labour services rendered them unnecessary. In most custumals look for a series of infinitive verbs depending on *debet* 'he must' or 'he is obliged' concerning the farming routine of the seasons, to harrow, sow, reap, etc.

Exercise 64

Translate

(a) *Idem debet metere in autumpno uno die cum uno homine et secundo die cum duobus hominibus sine cibo*
    The lord does not provide food

(b) *Et quelibet septimana operabili usque ad festum Sancti Petri ad Vincula debet operari per tres dies qualitercumque dominus voluerit*
    'each week of works' i.e. during every week in which he is obliged to work on the demesne; the scribe in this 12th-century document has used a classical deponent verb *operari* 'to perform the services due' where later medieval usage would have allowed *operare*; note the future perfect tense 'shall have wished'

(c) *Idem debet arare bis in yeme et semel in quadragesima*

(d) *Idem inveniet unum hominem ad levandum fenum uno toto die et cariabit duas carectatas feni ad orreum domini et debet sarcliare uno die contra festum nativitate sancti Johannis baptiste*
    Note the gerund followed by an accusative object after *ad*

(e) *Et singulis annis in vigilia sancti Martini ducere debet carucam suam ad locum ubi caruce domini arant et ibi arare debet unam acram et dimidiam*

If you want more information on court rolls, rentals and custumals consult the books listed in the appendix under 'For Further Reference'.

Chapter 6

Charters and Deeds

Deeds and charters are terms loosely used. The term charter is sometimes restricted to mean a written grant by a king or noble or other important person made to a town, institution or individual conferring or confirming some right or privilege such as borough status or the right to hold a market. Deeds are legal documents of any and every kind, amongst which title deeds, concerned with the ownership or occupation of landed property, are the most numerous and useful for research. Charters and deeds often have a similar structure and employ many of the same common-form expressions. Their length and the repetitious legal language in which they are sometimes couched may make them tedious to follow but they can be broken down into parts. Readers may wish to consult N.W. Alcock *Old Title Deeds* (Phillimore, 1986) which deals fully with this type of document in English.

Deeds of Gift

The accompanying annotated deed is a typical enfeoffment or deed of gift. Its structure should be studied closely. It consists of (1) an introduction in which the grantor commands everyone to know that he has done something (2) the name and title of the grantor in the nominative case (3) what he has done expressed by verbs such as 'given' and 'granted' in the perfect tense—the deed itself being a written confirmation of the action already performed (4) the name of the grantee, in the dative case (5) what is granted in the accusative case as the direct object of the verbs (6) further details amplifying or explaining the main grant introduced by the preposition *cum* and in the ablative case (7) often an *habendum* clause explaining the terms on which the property is to be held, e.g. paying and performing the due rents and services owed to the lord (8) a warranty clause by which the grantor guarantees, both for himself and his heirs, not to attempt to claim the property back (9) the grantor makes the grant even more permanent by affixing his deal (10) the *testimonium* or witnessing with the names of witnesses in the ablative case (11) the date and sometimes the place of the sealing of the deed.

Exercise 65

Summarise the annotated deed provided, giving the names of the grantor, grantee, description of main property granted, the terms on which the property is to be held, the names of the witnesses and the date and place.

Deeds of gift or a charter may begin with the grantor's name and include a salutation *Salutem* 'Greeting' from *salus, -utis* (f.), some such word as 'sends' being understood. The form of words in the introduction may vary but the verb is nearly always in the subjunctive:

A Feofment or Deed of Gift

Sciant presentes et futuri quod **Ego Radulphus miles dominus** de Grendon **dedi, concessi** et hac presenti carta mea **confirmavi domino Johanni** de Clynton, domino de Colleshull, totum **manerium** meum de Schenestan integre sine aliquo retenemento cum omnibus et singulis tenementis tenentium et tenementorum infra manerium predictum et extra, una cum homagiis, wardis, releviis heriotis, escheatis, sectis Curie, et cum tota terra arabili boscis, pratis, parcis, moris, pasturis, stagnis vivariis, piscariis, molendinis, aquis, viis semitis communiis, vastis, et cum omni dominio et donacione tam villanorum quam liberorum tenencium cum omnibus pertinenciis suis que de dictis terris et tenementis exigi poterunt quoque modo, una eciam cum tercia parte dotis que Isabella mater mea tenet in eodem manerio. **Tenendum et habendum, de capitali domino feodi illius,** predicto domino Johanni de Clinton et heredibus vel assignatis suis quibuscumque libere quiete integre bene in pace et jure hereditarie imperpetuum. **Reddendo et faciendo** inde annuatim Capitali domino feodi illius **servicia inde debita** et consueta, et michi et heredibus meis unum florem rose **ad festum nativitatis sancti Johannis Baptiste** pro omnibus serviciis secularibus exaccionibus et demandis universis. **Et ego predictus Radulphus de Grendon et heredes mei** predicto domino Johanni de Clynton et heredibus vel assignatis suis quibuscumque totum predictum manerium cum omnibus et singulis suis pertinenciis, ut supra plenius dictum est, contra omnes gentes **warantizabimus, acquietabimus, et defendemus imperpetuum.** Et ut hec mea donacio concessio et presentis carte mee, confirmacio rata et stabilis **permaneat,** eidem carte presenti sigillum meum apposui. **Hiis testibus,** Roberto de Pipa, Henrico Mauveysin, Johanne de Herumvile, militibus, Roberto de Barre, Villelmo de Tomenhorn, Willelmo de Freford, Willelmo Hary, Radulfo de Pipe, et aliis. Dat.' apud Sheneston die dominica proxima post festum Sancti Valentini Martiris anno regni regis Edwardi tercii vicesimo quarto

Introduction —— the grantor (nominative subject)

the grantee (dative case)

the main verbs (perfect tense)

all else in the grant (ablatives)

what is granted (direct object accusative case)

'habendum' clause (gerundives agreeing with 'manerium' accusative)

'of the chief lord of that fee'

acc. object of reddendo et faciendo

'by rendering and paying' (ablative gerunds)

time when payment is due

the grantor promises to support the title

the grantor strengthens the deed ('ut' plus subjunctive 'permaneat')

'these (being) witnesses' (ablative absolute)

the 'Testimonium' or acknowledgment of the deed with witnesses, date etc.

Exercise 65

Sciant omnes tam presentes quam futuri
Know all both present and future

Sciant is third person plural present subjunctive from *scio, scire, scivi, scitum* 'to know'

Pateat universis per presentia scripta
Let it be known to all (men) by the present writings

Pateat is a third person singular present subjunctive impersonal verb i.e. the subject is 'it'; *scripta* is neuter plural accusative after the preposition *per*; *presentia* is a present participle acting as an adjective and in agreement with *scripta*

Omnibus Christi fidelibus ad quos he littere pervenerint
To all Christ's faithful to whom these letters shall (have) come

Notum sit omnibus quod ego, Henricus ...
Let it be known to all that I, Henry ...

sit is present subjunctive third person singular of the verb *esse* 'to be' used here in an impersonal construction.

Usually a medieval deed used an Anglicised construction as above—*quod ego Henricus ...* and this is followed by verbs in the perfect tense and active voice *dedi, concessi* etc. Sometimes, the classical accusative and infinitive construction is employed.

Sciatis me Ranulphum dedisse civibus meis cartam ...
Know (ye) that I Ranulph have given a charter to my citizens
(Keep the translation in normal English)

The lands or other grants made by the main verbs may be further explained, defined or located:

dedi unum messuagium quod pater meus tenuit ...
I have given a messuage which my father held ...

concessi omnes terras quas habebam in Sotehulde
I have granted all the lands which I held in Sotehulde

Exercise 66
Translate

Sciant presentes et futuri quod ego Willelmus filius Radulphi de molendino reddidi in liberam et puram elemosinam priori et monachis de Tuttesburi duodecim acras terre in Merston in cultura que dicitur Apecroft quas Radulphus pater meus habuit de dono predictorum prioris et monachorum. Et ut hoc firmum sit et stabile cartam sigilli munime roboravi.

The *habendum* clause frequently found in title deeds usually takes the form of two gerundives, *habendum et tenendum,* meaning 'to have and to hold' and having the meaning of something which should be or is to be done. As verbal adjectives they agree in case, number and gender with the nouns to which they refer.

> *dedi terram habendam et tenendam Willelmo*
> I have given land to have and to hold to William

Here the gerundives are singular accusative feminine agreeing with *terram*

> *dedi unum messuagium et tres acras terre arabilis habenda et tenenda Willelmo*
> I have given a messuage and three acres of arable land to have and to hold to William

Here the gerundives are in the neuter plural accusative because they refer to nouns of different gender and number.

In practice the translation of such clauses will cause you no difficulty.

Quitclaims

The quitclaim, *quietumclamancia*, was the title deed by which lawyers endeavoured to close every loophole to any subsequent claim to a property by the grantor or by his 'heirs and assigns'. To identify quitclaims look for key words in the perfect tense such as *remisi, relaxavi* and *quietumclamavi*, or in the alternative accusative and infinitive construction, *remisisse, relaxasse, quietumclamasse.* Note that when the root of the perfect infinitive ends in *-v* the whole word may be shortened by the omission of *-vi-.* Look also for phrases such as *totum ius et clameum quod habui vel potui habere* 'all right and claim that I had or was able to have'.

Exercise 67

Translate

> *Sciant omnes tam presentes et futuri me Huctredum filium Nicholai de Brocton remisisse, relaxasse et quietumclamasse et hac carta mea confirmasse Roberto vicario de Dubbrig octo acras terre in territorio de Brocton ed dimidiam acram prati cum pertinenciis habendas et tenendas Robert sibi et assignatis et eorum heredibus reddendo inde annuatim domino priori de Tuttesburi et eiusdem loci conventui tres solidos et tres denarios scilicet ad festum sancti Johannis Baptiste octodecim denarios et ad festum sancti Michaelis decem et octo denarios et ad purificationem beate Marie iij denarios. Et ego vero Huctredus et heredes mei dictam terram cum messuagio in villa de Brocton contra omnes homines warantizabimus. In cuius rei testimonium huic presenti scripto sigillum meum apposui. Hiis testibus Johanne Welles, Rogero Turner et aliis.*

Not the plural accusative gerundives agreeing with *acras; sibi ... heredibus* 'to him and his assigns and their heirs'; *in cuius rei testimonium* 'in witness of which'

Exercise 68
Translate

> *Sciant presentes et futuri quod ego Robertus de Harekin concessi, relaxavi et quietumclamavi priori et conventui de Tuttesburi totum ius et clameum quod habui vel habere potui in crofto quod dicti prior et conventus emerunt de Gardino filio Ricardi sine reclamacione aliqua mei vel heredum meorum. Pro ista autem donacione concessione et quietaclamacione dederunt michi prior et monachi xx solidos sterlingorum*

emerunt third person plural perfect of *emo* 'to buy'; 'sterling' is often put into the genitive plural

Leases
Leases may start in the same was as deeds of gift but more typically with the phrase *Hac indentura facta inter ... '*. This indenture made between ...'. The term indenture refers to the way in which the document has been divided into two, one for each party to the lease, by an indented cut. Adopt the following procedure to translate: look for

- the name of the lessor in the nominative
- the name of the lessee in the dative
- a phrase by which to identify the document as a lease, e.g. *tradidi ad firmam* 'leased at farm' i.e. for rent
- the nature of the property being leased as a direct object of the main verbs, in the accusative
  any *habendum* clause followed by a name in the dative
- the term of the lease e.g. *ad quattuor annos* 'for 4 years'
- the term *reddendo* 'paying' and times of payment shown by reference to saints' days
- conditions or warnings attached to the lease—*si contingat* 'if it should happen'
- any warranty by the lessor
- the names of the witnesses

The start of different sections of the document may be signposted by large heavy letters.

Exercise 69
Translate

(a) *Hec indentura testatur quod ego Adam Banks tradidi ad firmam Elizabethe Miller unum cotagium iacens juxta communem viam HABENDUM ET TENENDUM sibi et heredibus suis libere quiete et in pace usque ad decem annos sequentes reddendo michi et heredibus vel assignatis meis duos solidos ad quattuor terminos anni per equales portiones. Et ego predictus Adam Banks et heredes mei totum illud cotagium prefate Elizabethe warantizabimus acquietabimus et defendemus contra omnes gentes IN CUIUS RE testimonium hiis scriptis indentatis sigillum meum apposui. Hiis testibus ...*

testatur 'witnesses' from *testor* (1 decl. deponent). Do not expect any modern punctuation in deeds

(b) *Et si contingat predictum redditum in toto vel in parte fore insolutum liceat predicto Ade heredibus et assignatis suis in toto tenemento predicto distringere*
fore is a form of the future infinitive; *liceat* 'let it be lawful' (subjunctive) is an impersonal verb which has only a third person singular in each tense; the lessor may distrain on the whole aforesaid tenement; *Ade* is dative of *Adam*.

(c) *Et si contingat predictum redditum in parte vel in toto ad aliquem terminum aretro fore insolutum liceat prefato Ade illud tenementum ingredi et possidere sine contradicione*
aretro 'in arrears'; *ingredi* (3 conj. dep.) 'to enter'

Bargain and Sale

This was a form of conveyance much used after its creation by the Statute of Enrolments of 1535. Provided it was enrolled in a royal court or at county quarter sessions it was legally valid without the need for the ceremony of 'livery of seisin', the symbolic handing over of a piece of turf or a stick in the presence of witnesses. Look for a series of perfect infinitives which include *vendidisse* 'to have sold' and *barganizasse*, 'to have bargained'. Such documents are difficult only because of the complexity of the subordinate clauses and phrases which describe the lands and their appurtenances and the conditions of tenure in repetitive detail. The Bargain and Sale document in the next exercise has had much detail edited out.

Exercise 70

Translate

> *OMNIBUS CHRISTI FIDELIBUS ad quos presens scriptum indentatum pervenerit Hugo Jones de civitate London mercer Salutem in domino sempiternam ... NOVERITIS me prefatum Hugonem Jones pro quadam summa pecunie mihi per Thomam Powntes de Longdon in comitatu Staffordie soluta VENDIDISSE barganizasse feoffasse concessisse et hoc presenti scripto indentato confirmasse prefato Thome Powntes illas terras in Longdon vocatas Churchelandes ... HABENDAS TENENDAS ET GAUDENDAS omnia et singula premissa cum pertinenciis prefato Thome Powntes heredibus et assignatis suis in perpetuum ... ET EGO VERO prefatus Hugo Jones et heredes mei omnia premissa cum suis pertinenciis prefato Thome Powntes heredibus et assignatis suis contra me et heredes meos warantizabimus et imperpetuum defendemus per presentes ... IN CUIUS REI TESTIMONIUM ego predictus Hugo Jones ... et Thomas Powntes ... his Indenturis sigilla nostra alternatim apposuimus datum vicesimo die Septembris anno regni domine nostre Elizabethe vicesimo quarto*

Noveritis is 3 conj. 2 pers. plur. perf. subj. from *nosco, -ere, novi, notum* a defective verb i.e. lacking a number of forms and meaning 'to get to know'. Translate as 'Know (ye)'. Note the extra gerundive *gaudendas* agreeing with *terras* plur. acc.

Final Concords

The final concord or fine derives its name from the opening phrase *Hec est finalis concordia* 'This is the final agreement' of a document recording a case in the Court of Common Pleas. It was not possible under medieval land law to register a title to property so landowners had recourse to a fictitious action at law. A typical example is where the plaintiff *querens* who is the actual buyer of the property brings an action against the defendant *deforciator* on the grounds that the latter is in illegal possession of the property. With the agreement of the court they settle the dispute by a final concord. This was duly recorded and thus the two parties have succeeded in getting the title to the property registered. The document was prepared in triplicate and was then divided into three. The third part, known as the Foot, was retained by the court, and these Feet of Fines now survive mainly in the Public Record Office. The financial details and measurements given in the document are not to be trusted, but names, locations and dates are of use to the local and family historian.

In the following fine for translation, the property is described as 'ten acres of meadow'; the defendants recognise the right of the plaintiff and remise and quitclaim the property to him. Persevere with the translation, despite its tediousness, because of the useful vocabulary and grammar.

Exercise 71
Translate

> *Hec est finalis concordia facta in Curia Domine Regine apud Westmonasterium in crastino Sancte Trinitatis anno regni Domine Elizabethe dei gratia Anglie Francie et Hibernie Regine fidei defensoris a conquestu vicesimo nono coram Edwardo Anderson, Francisco Wyndham justiciariis et aliis domine regine fidelibus tunc ibi presentibus inter Robertum Baker querentem et Willelmum Mascall et Agnetem uxorem eius deforciatores de decem acris prati cum pertinenciis in Denham unde placitum convencionis summonitum fuit inter eos in eadem curia scilicet quod predicti Willelmus et Agnes recognoverunt predictum tenementum cum pertinenciis esse ius ipsius Roberti Baker ut illi que idem Robertus habuit de dono predictorum Willelmi Mascall et Agnetis et illi remiserunt et quietumclamaverunt de ipsis Willelmo et Agnete et heredibus predicto Roberto et heredibus suis imperpetuum. Et preterea iidem Willelmus et Agnes concesserunt pro se et heredibus ipsius Willelmi quod ipsi warantizabunt predicto Roberto Baker et heredibus suis predictum tenementum contra omnes imperpetuum. Et pro hac recognitione remissione quietaclamancia warantia fine et concordia idem Robertus Baker dedit predictis Willelmo Mascall et Agneti octoginta libras sterlingorum.*

facta 'made' past participle passive agrees with *concordia*; English monarchs continued to claim the throne of France until the Treaty of Amiens 1802; the preposition *coram* takes an ablative; *unde ... fuit* 'concerning which a plea of covenant was summoned'; *ut ... dono* 'as being that which the said Robert has of the gift of'; note the string of ablatives after *pro*.

Town Charters

Charters conferring rights or privileges to the citizens of towns have the same basic structure as deeds of gift. The subjunctive verb of command is usually accompanied by an accusative and infinitive construction; *quod* introduces a series of verbs in the subjunctive, citing the rights which the citizens are to enjoy quietly etc. Sometimes there is an additional clause imposing a penalty on anyone who attempts to disturb the grantees in these rights.

Exercise 72

Translate this charter of 1235 (which has been slightly shortened)

> *Henricus dei gratia Rex Anglie Dominus Hibernie et Dux Aquitainie, archiepiscopis episcopis abbatibus prioribus comitibus baronibus justiciariis vicecomitibus prepositis ministris et omnibus ballivis et fidelibus Salutem. SCIATIS nos concessisse et hac carta nostra confirmasse ... burgensibus de Novo Castro subtus Lymam quod villa nostra de Novo Castro sit liber burgus et quod burgenses eiusdem ville habeant gildam mercatorum in eodem burgo cum omnibus libertatibus ... ad huismodi gildam pertinentibus ... et quod eant per totam terram nostram cum omnibus mercandisis suis emendo et vendendo ... in pace libere et quiete ... Hiis testibus Guillielmo de Ferraris Galfrido Despensatore et aliis. Datum per manum venerabilis Patris Radulphi Cicestrensis episcopi Cancellarii nostri apud Feckeham decimo octavo die Septembris anno regni nostri decimo nono.*

sit liber burgus 'may be a free borough'; *eant* they may go' (pres. subj. 3 pers. plur. of *eo* 'to go'); note the dative gerunds 'for buying and selling'

Exercise 73

Translate this charter in which the Earl of Chester granted the citizens of that city a monopoly of the right to trade in goods brought there except during specified fairs.

> *Sciatis me concessisse dominicis hominibus Cestrie et eorum heredibus quod nullus aliquod genus mercimonii ad civitatem Cestrie per mare aut per terram venerit emat aut vendat nisi ipsi aut eorum heredes aut per eorum gratum nisi in nundinis assisis in nativitate Sancti Johannis Baptiste et in festo Sancti Michaelis. Quare volo quod predicti homines mei et eorum heredes habeant et teneant predictam libertatem de me et de heredibus meis imperpetuum libere, quiete, honorifice et pacifice. Et prohibeo super forisfacturam decem librarum ad opus meum capiendarum ne aliquis eos super dictam libertatem impediat aut gravet.*

dominicus hominibus 'to the demesne men'; *nullus* is the subject and *genus* the direct object of the verbs *emat* and *vendat; ad opus meum capiendarum* has a gerundive in the genitive plural

Chapter 7

Abbreviations in Latin Local History Documents

Formal documents such as royal charters are written out in full but in many other types of local history document, especially ecclesiastical and manorial records, the Latin is heavily abbreviated as the medieval scribes sought to save parchment and time. The abbreviations and conventions they used were of standard form, and the vocabulary was so familiar that reading the documents presented no difficulty. In general the scribes 'played fair': if they abbreviated a word they indicated this by some mark. Any individual style or quirks a scribe may display will soon become apparent to the modern researcher.

Abbreviation marks fall into four types, dealt with under the headings below.

1 General Marks of Suspension and Contractions

Suspension is the omission of the final letter/s of a word with a mark used to indicate such omission. This takes the form of a straight, curved or wavy horizontal line above the letters which are written.

cū or *cũ* =	*cu(m)* 'with'	*nat̂* = *nat(ivitas)* 'birth'.

Obviously the abbreviated words must be extended differently according to the case-ending or verb-ending required. Thus *nat̂* above might have been extended into *nat̂(ivitatem)* accusative, *nat(ivitatis)* genitive, etc. Without a knowledge of grammar it would be impossible to make these extensions accurately.

In some suspensions the omission of letters may be indicated by a line continuing from the last letter written and in the case of 'm' and 'n' often curving up and back.

habendꝛ = *habend(um)* This has been extended to make a gerund; obviously it could have been a gerundive, habend(a), habend(am), habend(as) etc.

man̄ = (for example) *man(erium)*, *man(erio)* etc.

Contraction means that some letters in the middle of a word have been omitted and this is also indicated by a straight or wavy line over. Sometimes this line will pass through an ascender of 'd', 'b', 'h' or 'l'.

Rogūs	=	*Rog(er)us* 'Roger'
Johēs	=	*Joh(ann)es* 'John'
balłīo	=	*balliv(v)o* 'bailiff' (ablative).

A flourish at the end of a word may also indicate that some letters have been omitted

armigi⁾   =   *armig(er)i* 'esquire' (here the word from which this sign was reproduced was a genitive)

pannag⁾   =   *pannag(io)* 'pannage' (here it was ablative)

A mark rather like a cursive 'e' with a long tail may be found in early documents used as a general mark of abbreviation but later it was restricted to represent a terminal -*es* or -*is*

Milite   =   *Milit(is)* 'knight' (genitive)

2   Modification of letters to indicate abbreviation

When the descender of the letter 'p' has a bar which starts as a separate stroke or from the bottom of the descender it indicates *p(er)* or *p(ar)*   *p* *p*

sup   =   *sup(er)* 'on' (prep. +acc.)
pte   =   *p(ar)te* 'side' (abl.)

When the bar through the descender starts from the top of the letter or from the looper of the '*p*' and curls back to the left before crossing the descender it indicates the omission of -*ro*

p   =   *p(ro)* 'for' (prep. + abl.)
put   =   *p(ro)ut* 'according as' (adv.)

The mark *2* looking rather like an Arabic 2 with an oblique line through the tail stands for -*rum*, the genitive plural case-ending

porco2   =   *porco(rum)* 'of the pigs'
terra2   =   *terra(rum)* 'of the lands'

A mark consisting of a backward curve ending in a bold pendent comma, though always retaining its use as a general mark of abbreviation, was also used from the 13th century to indicate the omission of -*re* especially after '*p*'

p'dcm̄   =   *p(re)d(i)c(tu)m* aforesaid (there are two marks of abbreviation here; the past participle *predictus* in all its forms was so much used that it was often reduced to two letters *p'd-* and when extending you must ensure the correct agreement with the noun referred to).

3   Abbreviation by superior letters

A letter or letters written above the normal level of the line of writing usually signifies the omission of two or more letters of which the superior letter is one. Such an abbreviation mark often follows '*q*'

$q^e rela$ = $q(ue)rela$ 'suit/action' (legal)

$q^a d\bar{a}$ = $q(ua)dam(m)$ 'a certain (person/thing)' (pron., here in abl. case, f. gender, from *quidam, quedam, quoddam*)

A superior *'a'* often extended at the top indicates the omission of *-ra*

$cont^a$ = $cont(ra)$ 'against' ('before' in expressions of time)

$t^a xit$ = $t(ra)xit$ 'drew' (3 pers. perf. of *traho, -ere, traxi, tractum* (3) found in manorial court rolls recording an assault *traxit sanguinem* 'he drew blood')

4 Marks significant in themselves actually indicating which letters are missing

A sign rather like the Arabic numeral 9 placed at the beginning of a word and on the line means *con-*

$_9querens$ =   *(con)querens* 'plaintiff'

If this sign is used as a superior terminal letter it represents *-us*

$temp^9$ = $temp(us)$ 'time' (*tempus, -oris* n.)

op^9 = $op(us)$ 'work' (*opus, operis* n.)

A sign that looks rather like a modern cursive 'z' or an Arabic numeral 3 with a slightly extended tail usually abbreviates three classes of words, (i) those with the dative or ablative plural ending *-bus*, in which the sign stands for the last two letters, (ii) those ending in *-que* in which it represents the *-ue*, and (iii) those ending in *-et* in which it replaces these letters.

heredib3   =   *heredib(us)* 'heirs' (dat. or abl. plur.)

usq3   =   *usq(ue)* 'as far as' (adv.); note how the tail of the abbreviation mark crosses the tail of the *'q'*

ut^{m}q3   =   *ut(ram)q(ue)* 'each' (f. acc. of *uterque, utraque, utrumque;* note also abbreviation by superior letter)

ten3   =   *ten(et)* 'he holds'

The *-ur* or *-tur* ending of the verb in the third person present, future and imperfect passive is represented by a sign not unlike an Arabic numeral 2 which follows the last letter and is almost invariably written above the line *saisiat*^{2} = *saisiat(ur)* 'is seized'

ponit^{2} = *ponit(ur)* 'is put'

There are also a number of abbreviations which do not fit into the categories above. These include ampersands (the abbreviation of 'and' and still used in English &) and which in medieval hands are found in a variety of forms. A few of these are

⁊ ⁊ ⁊ = *et* 'and'

'et cetera' is often represented by ⁊c

J̅h̅s̅ X̅p̅s̅ J̅h̅c̅ X̅p̅c̅ stand for 'Jesus (Christ)'.

In very early documents you may find the verb *est* 'is' represented by a symbol that looks like the arithmetical sign of division ÷

Exercise 74

Extend the following abbreviated words and phrases putting your extensions within brackets, then translate

(a) *cū om̄ibʒ aliis*
(b) *p*^{2}*fatū tenem̄tum*
(c) *ubiqʒ*
(d) *imp̱petuū*
(e) *libē quiete bn̄ ⁊ in pace*
(f) *in cui⁹ rei testimoniū*
(g) *hiis testibʒ Joh̄e Proudfoot tunc ballīō, Waltō tinctore*

Record Type

From the late 18th century and up to about 1900 a special fount called Record Type was used to attempt to reproduce in print the abbreviation marks and symbols used in medieval manuscripts, and a considerable number of records were published in this print. The text of *Domesday Book*, printed in this type in 1783 has been reproduced by Phillimore the publishers of this book, beginning in 1975, with translations of the facing page, and is particularly useful for beginners wishing to familiarise themselves with the medieval system of abbreviation. The obvious drawback is that such transcriptions tend to over-rationalise the scribes' use of abbreviation marks. The following exercises demonstrate the utility and difficulties of using Record Type transcriptions.

Exercise 75

With the aid of the translations provided transcribe the following, extending the abbreviated words and putting the extensions within brackets. Full notes provided for the first exercise only. Use the glossary and the tables in the appendix.

(a)   HUG' LE P'TER recupavit in cuᵲ plena vj hoꝉ fᵲi ꝉ j qᵗrᵲ aveñ
de Ioñ Karles ad solvenꝺ in festo ƀi Micñ aᵒ xxiiijᵒ . ad hoc fideⁱᵲ
solvenꝺ Invenit pleḡ Henᵲ de Ford ꝉ·Raꝺ de Peck.

Hugh le Porter recovered in full court 6 hoppers of wheat and one quarter
of oats from John Karles to be paid at the feast of St. Michael in the 24th
year; for faithfully paying this he found pledges Henry de Ford and Ralph de
Peck

- did you make the extension of the abbreviated '*p*' in the word meaning 'recovered'?
- the adjective *plena* agrees with its noun *cur(ia)*
- 'hoppers' and 'quarter' must be in the accusative case as direct objects of 'recovered'; one superscript omission and one suspension in 'quarter'
- (of) 'wheat' must be genitive
- 'John' is ablative after *de*; remember '*I*' and '*J*' are interchangeable
- for *ad solvenꝺ* turn back, if necessary, to the section on gerunds
- the translation 'Michaelmas' would be acceptable
- another superscript letter, this time a contraction with two middle letters omitted; remember ablative case for time when
- we are not told whose 24th year this is—the monarch? the year of office of an abbot?
- another gerund now
- *Invenit* could be present tense or perfect
- what case must *pleḡ* be in as the direct object of *Invenit*?
- Henry and Radulph are in apposition to 'pledges' so make their extensions grammatically correct

Not a really difficult transcription of the abbreviated Latin, you agree? Now try the next exercise; not so much help provided!

(b)   Pñ Pistor debet ixs. vjꝺ. Riᶜ Meysey Iᵗ debꝫ iijs. vjꝺ.
Matheo de Lodelowe Iᵗ dꝫ ꝺno ijs. vjꝺ.   Iᵗ vjꝺ.   Iᵗ Martiñ Parcaᵲ
vjs. vjꝺ.   Iᵗ xiiijꝺ. Enoᶜ de Novo Castᵲ—qᵃᵲ adjudicatᵘˢ est adᵲ
carcerᵉ quousqꝫ solvit totū vel invenᵏit pleḡ . Iᵗ dꝫ xxꝺ. Haniᵏ
quos solvit ꝑ pleḡ ejᵘˢdm.

Philip the Baker owes 9s.6d. to Richard Meysey. Likewise he owes 3s.6d. to
Matthew of Ludlow. Likewise he owes the lord 2s.6d. Likewise 6d. Likewise
to Martin Parker 6s.6d. Likewise 14d. to Enoch of Newcastle—wherefore he
is condemned to prison until he pays the whole or finds (literally 'shall have
found') pledges. Likewise he owes 20d. to Hanik which he paid for his pledge
(literally 'for the pledge of the same').

- line 2 notice how the straight abbreviation mark over '(to) the lord' goes through the ascender of the '*d*'

- datives for both parts of the name 'Martin Parker'; this document dates from the 14th century when surnames were evolving and occupational names like 'the Baker' and 'the Parker' were losing the definite article.
- line 3 provides an example of a good Record Type abbreviation, the superior mark ^{9} meaning -us
- line 4 *quousq(ue)*
- *solvit* has the same form for 3 pers. present and perfect; let the context be your guide.

(c)

Elizabeth by the grace of god of England France and Ireland Queen defender of the faith etc. To all to whom our present letters shall come, Greeting. Know ye that Robert Donnington in our Court before our judges at Westminster sued Robert Hammerton and Margery his wife concerning etc.

- line 3 Notice the Record Type marks for the two contractions in 'shall have come'
- *impli(ci)tavit* 'impleaded' i.e. 'sued'
- the legal formula in this summary has been reduced to (an abbreviated) *et cetera*

Consult the books listed in the appendix to extend your knowledge of and acquaintance with medieval Latin palaeography, then try something of your own that no one else has ever attempted. You will get a thrill from your success.

Answers
to
Exercises

Exercise 1

edifico, edificas, edificat, edificamus, edificatis, edificant   (build)

laboro, laboras, laborat, laboramus, laboratis, laborant   (work)

voco, vocas, vocat, vocamus, vocatis, vocant   (call)

assigno, assignas, assignat, assignamus, assignatis, assignant   (assign)

contento, contentas, contentat, contentamus, contentatis, contentant   (pay)

Exercise 2

Rome, land, moon, daughter, island, letter, life, charter, parson, parish, church, pasture, rope, queen, Julia

Exercise 3

(a) He (pronoun); surrendered (verb); the (def. art.); tenement (noun); into (preposition); hands (noun); of (preposition); lord (noun)

(b) jury (noun); say (verb); he (pronoun); is (verb); not (adverb); guilty (adjective)

(c) court (noun); was held (verb); on (preposition); Monday (noun); after (adverb); feast (noun); of (preposition); St. James (noun)

Exercise 4

(a) lord (noun, nominative); readily (adverb); grants (verb); a (indefinite article); charter (noun, accusative); to (preposition); borough (noun, dative)

(b) John Wodard (noun, nominative); comes (verb); into (preposition); court (noun, accusative if motion is involved, ablative if it denotes rest); and (conjunction); does (verb); fealty (noun, accusative as direct object of verb)

(c) He (pronoun, nominative); holds (verb); one (numeral adjective because it qualifies 'care'); acre (noun, accusative, direct object of verb); villein (normally a noun but here used as an adjective qualifying 'land'); in (preposition); manor (noun, ablative of place where); Berham (noun, genitive because preceded by 'of')

(d) By (preposition); this (here an adjective qualifying, and therefore in the same case as, 'charter'); charter (noun, ablative of instrument or means), we (pronoun, nominative subject of 'confirm'); confirm (verb); grant (noun, accusative, object of 'confirm'); tithes (noun, genitive); to (preposition); church (noun, dative for person to whom something is given)

(e) defendant (noun, nominative); unjustly (adverb); raised (verb); hue and cry (nouns, accusative, object of 'raised')

(f) I (pronoun, nominative); affix (verb); my (possessive adjective, accusative qualifying 'seal'); seal (noun, accusative object of verb); to (preposition); will (noun, dative).

Exercise 5
(a) The queen gives (the) land to the parish
(b) The king gives the charter to the parson
(c) The king confirms the land by (a) charter
(d) The lord seizes the land of the church
(e) I give a cow to the girl
(f) The lord holds an acre of land in the parish

Exercise 6
(a) The lord neither gives nor confirms the charter
     Dominus (nom. sing.), *cartam* (acc. sing.)
(b) Both the parson and the lord have pasture in the land
     parsona (nom. sing.) *dominus* (nom. sing.), *pasturam* (acc. sing.), *terra* (abl. sing.)
(c) The parson gives a cow and land to the daughter of the farmer
     Parsona (nom. sing.), *vaccam* (acc. sing.), *terram* (acc. sing.), *filie* (dat. sing.),
     agricole (gen. sing.)

Exercise 7
(a) The king gives lands to the churches
     Rex (nom. sing.), *ecclesiis* (dat. plur.), *terras* (acc. plur.)
(b) The lord seizes the lands of the farmers
     Dominus (nom. sing.), *terras* (acc. plur.). *agricolarum* (gen. plur.)
(c) Julia, daughter of the parson, holds a tenement with 2 acres of land
     Julia (nom. sing.), *filia* (nom. sing.), *parsone* (gen. sing.), *tenementum* (acc. sing.),
     acris (abl. plur.), *terre* (gen. sing.)

Exercise 8
filia 'daughter', *vacca* 'cow', *carta* 'charter', *pastura* 'pasture', *bosca* 'wood', *curia* 'court',
villa 'township', *fossa* 'dike'

	Singular	Plural	Singular	Plural
Nom.	*filia*	*filie*	*vacca*	*vacce*
Voc.	*filia*	*filie*	*vacca*	*vacce*
Acc.	*filiam*	*filias*	*vaccam*	*vaccas*
Gen.	*filie*	*filiarum*	*vacce*	*vaccarum*
Dat.	*filie*	*filiabus**	*vacce*	*vaccis*
Abl.	*filia*	*filiabus**	*vacca*	*vaccis*

     * the dative and ablative plural of *filia* takes *-abus* to avoid confusion with the
     dat. and abl. plur. of *filius* (m. 2nd Declension 'son')

Exercise 9
(a) We, the king and queen, seize the lands of the church
(b) The lord out of (his) favour confirms a charter to the church
(c) When are you confirming the charter?
(d) When art thou (are you) paying the money to the parson?
(e) The church holds one acre in the parish

Exercise 10

year, boy, messuage, place, reign, field, manor

	Singular	Plural	Singular	Plural	Singular	Plural
Nom.	*annus*	*anni*	*puer*	*pueri*	*messuagium*	*messuagia*
Voc.	*anne*	*anni*	*puer*	*pueri*	*messuagium*	*messuagia*
Acc.	*annum*	*annos*	*puerum*	*pueros*	*messuagium*	*messuagia*
Gen.	*anni*	*annorum*	*pueri*	*puerorum*	*messuagii*	*messuagiorum*
Dat.	*anno*	*annis*	*puero*	*pueris*	*messuagio*	*messuagiis*
Abl.	*anno*	*annis*	*puero*	*pueris*	*messuagio*	*messuagiis*

Exercise 11

(a) The lord holds a manor court (court of the manor)
(b) The king gives a charter to the borough
(c) We give money to the slaves
(d) We, Robert and Henry, assign 10 acres of land in the parish to the church of Saint Peter
(e) You give a virgate of land to the church
(f) I give lands to William's son and confirm by a charter
(g) The lord seizes the messuages with the lands of the farmers in the manor
(h) The steward assigns pastures and woods in the manor to the villeins

Exercise 12

(a) Great court with view of frankpledge of the lord Henry de Ferrers
Curia (nom., sing., fem., subject), *domini* (gen., sing., masc.); *Henrici* (gen., sing., masc.); *visu* (abl., sing., masc. after preposition *cum*), *franciplegij* (gen., sing., masc.)
(b) View of frankpledge held on the morrow of Saint Matthew
Visus (nom., sing., masc., subject); *franciplegij* (gen., sing., masc.); *crastino* (abl., sing., neut., after preposition *in*); *Sancti* (gen., sing., masc.); *Matthei* (gen., sing., masc.)
(c) The parson pays 3 shillings rent
Parsona (nom., sing., masc., subject); *solidos* (acc., plural, masc., direct object of *solvit*); *redditum* (acc., sing., masc., also direct object of *solvit*)
(d) To this court comes William Lathropp of Legh in the county of Stafford and surrenders into the hands of the lord of the aforesaid manor half of two messuages
curiam (acc., sing., fem. after preposition *ad*); *Willelmus* (nom., sing., masc., subject); *Legh* (no case shown, probably abl., after *de*); *comitatu* (abl., sing., masc. after preposition *in*); *Staffordie* (gen., sing., fem.); *manus* (acc., plur., fem., after *in*); *domini* (gen., sing., masc.); *manerij* (gen., sing., neut.); *medietatem* (acc., sing., fem., direct object of *sursumreddit,* see Chap.3 for 3rd declension forms); *messuagiorum* (gen., plur., neut.)
(e) Richard of Potlak holds one burgage and pays 12d. to the abbot
Ricardus (nom., sing., masc., subject); *burgagium* (acc., sing., neut., direct object of *tenet*); *d.* = *denarios* (acc., plur., masc., direct object of *solvit*); *abbati* (dat., sing., masc. indirect object of *solvit*)

(f)   Elena daughter of Walter (the) carpenter holds a meadow near Skyrem Meadow
      Elena, filia (nom., sing., fem. subjects in apposition); *Walteri* (gen., sing., masc.);
      carpentarij (gen., sing., masc.), *pratum* (acc., sing., neut., direct object of *tenet*),
      Skyrem Medwe (English placename, no Latin form shown)

Exercise 13
(a)   The king gives good land to the church
      bonam (acc., sing., fem. agreeing with *terram*)
(b)   The lord assigns lands to the good serf
      bono (dat., sing., masc., agreeing with *servo*)
(c)   The land of the lord has many cows
      multas (acc. plur., fem., agreeing with *vaccas*)
(d)   The lord confirms the charter to the aforesaid borough
      predicto (dat., sing., masc., agreeing with *burgo*)
(e)   We give money to the good serfs
      bonis (dat., plur., masc., agreeing with *servis*)
(f)   The lord William seizes the lands of the aforesaid parson
      predicti (gen., sing., masc., agreeing with *parsone*)
(g)   We, the aforesaid Edward and Elizabeth, assign ten acres of land in our manor to
      the church of Saint Modwen
      predicti (nom., plur., masc.) agreeing with *Edwardus* and *Elizabetha decem* (numeral
      adj. does not decline); *nostro* (abl., sing., neut., agreeing with *manerio*)

Exercise 14
(a)   I, Richard, confirm to the church of Saint Leonard all the land with appurte-
      nances
      Ego (pronoun, nom., sing., applicable to all genders, subject); *Ricardus* (nom.,
      sing., masc., subject); *ecclesie* (dat., sing., fem., indirect object); *Sancti Leonardi*
      (gen., sing., masc.); *totam* (acc., sing., fem., agreeing with *terram*); *terram* (acc.,
      sing., fem., direct object); *pertinenciis* (abl., plur., fem. after *cum*)
(b)   The king gives to the lord one acre of meadow out of [his] lands
      Rex (nom., sing., masc., subject); *domino* (dat., sing., masc., indirect object); *unam*
      (adjective, acc., sing., fem., agreeing with *acram*); *acram* (acc., sing., fem., direct
      object of verb *dat*); *prati* (gen., sing., neut.); *terris* (abl., plur., fem., after prepo-
      sition *e*)
(c)   The court held on Monday next after the feast of Saint Barnabas
      Curia (nom., sing., fem., subject); *die* (abl., sing., masc.); *Lune* (gen., sing., fem.);
      proximo (adj., sing., masc., agreeing with *die*); *festum* (sing., neut., after preposi-
      tion *post*); *Sancti Barnabe* (gen., sing. NB *Barnabe* has fem. form but is masc.)
(d)   The court held on Tuesday in the feast of Saint Juliana
      Curia (nom., sing., fem., subject); *die* (abl., sing., masc., time); *Martis* (gen., sing.,
      masc.); *festo* (abl., sing., neut., after preposition *in*); *Sancte Juliane* (gen., sing.,
      fem.)
(e)   Nicholas Bond appears in court against Henry and Alice
      Nicolaus Bond (nom., sing., masc., subject); *se* (reflexive pronoun, acc., sing., or

plur.) *Henricum* (acc., sing., masc. after preposition *versus*); *Aliciam* (acc., sing., fem., after *versus*)

(f)   Elena raises the hue-and-cry against Radulph
      Elena (nom., sing., fem., subject); *hutesium* (acc., sing., neut., direct object); *Radulphum* (acc., sing., masc. after preposition *super*)

Exercise 15

well, freely, quietly, falsely, best, briefly, easily

Exercise 16

(a)   Matilda unjustly raised the hue-and-cry
(b)   He holds the tenement freely and quietly forever (in perpetuity)
(c)   Robert pays annually 2 shillings at the term of Saint Martin
(d)   John le Bonde carries two cartloads as far as Bronston
(e)   Henry must hoe for one day without food (i.e. provided by the lord) before the feast of Saint Peter
(f)   Samuel Emery and Samuel his son hold a parcel of land near the royal highway

Exercise 17

video 'to see', *iaceo* 'to lie' (also found as *jaceo*), *maneo* 'to remain', *moveo* 'to move', *sedeo* 'to sit'

> *video, vides, videt, videmus, videtis, vident*
> *iaceo, iaces, iacet, iacemus, iacetis, iacent*

Exercise 18

(a)   One acre lies in the meadow
(b)   I see the parson in the church
(c)   The church holds 3 rods (square measure as well as linear) in the manor
(d)   William and Alice his wife hold 3 messuages at the will of the lord

Exercise 19

occupo 'to seize, occupy'; *assigno* 'to assign'; *condono* 'to excuse'; *presento* 'to present' (i.e. make a presentment of an offender, present information); *warantizo* 'to warrant' (i.e. guarantee)

> *occupavi, occupavisti, occupavit, occupavimus, occupavistis, occupaverunt*
> *assignavi, assignavisti, assignavit, assignavimus, assignavistis, assignaverunt*

Exercise 20

moneo 'to warn'; *habeo* 'to have'; *debeo* 'to owe' (i.e. money; when followed by an infinitive means 'to be obliged to do something)

> *monui, monuisti, monuit, monuimus, monuistis, monuerunt*
> *habui, habuisti, habuit, habuimus, habuistis, habuerunt*

Exercise 21

(a) On which day he appeared (i.e. before the court) and the judge warned him
die (abl., sing., fem., time); *dominus* (nom., sing., masc., subject); *eum* (pronoun, acc., sing., masc., direct object of verb *monuit*)

(b) Sewinus the smith held 4 acres of land in the manor
Sewinus faber (nom., sing., masc., subjects in apposition); *acras* (acc., plur., fem., direct object of *tenuit*); *terre* (gen., sing., fem.); *manerio* (abl., sing., neut. after preposition *in*, place where)

(c) I, Bertram de Verdun, for (the sake of) my soul and for the soul of Rohais my wife have given all the land of Croxden to God and to the blessed Mary and by this charter have confirmed it
Ego (nom., sing., masc., pronoun, subject of verb *dedi*); *Bertram de Verdun* (nom., sing., masc., subject), *anima* (abl., sing., fem., following preposition *pro*); *mea* (abl., sing., fem., adjective in agreement with *anima*); *Rohais* (no case shown for this name, but in a Latin form would have been gen., sing., fem.); *uxoris* (gen., sing., fem., of 3rd declension noun, see later in chapter 2); *mee* (gen., sing., fem., adjective, agreeing with *uxoris*); *totam* (acc., sing., fem., adjective agreeing with *terram*); *terram* (acc., sing., fem., direct object of *dedi*); *Croxden* (no case shown, would have been abl., sing., gender uncertain); *deo* (dat., sing., masc., indirect object of *dedi*); *Marie* (dat., sing., fem., indirect object); *beate* (dat., sing., fem., adjective agreeing with *Marie*); *hac* (abl., sing., fem., adjective agreeing with *carta*); *carta* (abl., sing., fem., agent)

(d) Adam the tanner owes appearance (at court) and has not come and the court fined him 6d. for default of court (attendance)
Adam tannator (nom., sing., masc. subjects in apposition); *apparentiam* (acc., sing., fem., direct object of verb *debet*); *curia* (nom., sing., fem., subject) *eum* (acc., sing., masc., pronoun, direct object of *amerciavit*); *denarios* (acc., plur., masc., also direct object of *amerciavit*); *defalta* (abl., sing., fem., after preposition *pro*); *curie* (gen., sing., fem.)

Exercise 22

(a) The farmer ploughed his lands
Agricola (nom., sing., masc. with fem. form, subject); *terras* (acc., plur., fem.); *suas* (acc., plur., fem., adjective agreeing with *terras*)

(b) The king gave land in the parish to the lord
Rex (nom., sing., masc., subject); *domino* (dat., sing., masc., indirect object); *terram* (acc., sing., fem., direct object); *parochia* (abl., sing., fem., following preposition *in*)

(c) We, William and Elizabeth, have confirmed 9 acres of pasture to William our son
Nos (nom., plur., both genders, subject); *Willelmus* (nom., sing., masc., subject); *Elizabetha* (nom., sing., fem., subject); *ix* (*novem;* num., adj.; cardinal nos. indeclinable from 4 to 100); *acras* (acc., plur., fem., direct object); *pasture* (gen., sing., fem.); *Willelmo* (dat., sing., masc., indirect object); *filio* (dat., sing., masc., indirect object, in apposition to *Willelmo*); nostro (dat., sing., masc., possessive pronoun used only as adjective)

(d) Know all (men) that I, John, have given and by this charter confirmed 10 rods of
     meadow to the church of Saint Peter
     omnes (nom., plur., both genders, subject); *ego, Johannes* (nom., sing., masc.,
     subject of *dedi*); *prati* (gen., sing., neut.); *ecclesie* (dat., sing., fem., indirect object);
     Sancti Petri (gen., sing., masc.); *hac* (abl., sing., fem., adjective agreeing with
     carta); *carta* (abl., sing., fem., agent)
(e) Richard and Radulph have given to the monks of Tutbury in perpetuity the claim
     which they had in the pasture of Ednulston
     Ricardus and *Radulphus* (nom., plur., masc. subjects); *clameum* (acc., sing., neut.,
     direct object); *pastura* (abl., sing., fem., after *in Ednulston* (no case shown); *monachis*
     (dat., plur., masc., indirect object); *Tuttesbir* (no case shown)

Exercise 23

(a) The villeins ploughed the fields on the morrow of Saint Martin
(b) We held one meadow in the aforesaid borough
(c) I, John of Halton, Esquire, have given and by this my charter have confirmed to
     Henry son of Thomas the porter those lands which I held in the park
(d) William son of Nicholas holds one messuage with a curtilage and pays to the
     almoner 2s.6d.

Exercise 24

(a) And I and my heirs will warrant and acquit the aforesaid tenement to the afore-
     said William in perpetuity
(b) The lord gave the lands which he held in the parish to the church
(c) The monks will pray for the soul of lord Radulph

Exercise 25

wife, Trinity, Assumption, abbot, gift, salvation/greeting

uxor, uxor, uxorem, uxoris, uxori, uxore
Trinitas, Trinitas, Trinitatem, Trinitatis, Trinitati, Trinitate (no plur.)

Exercise 26

work or customary service or use, body, right

(Sing.)	*opus, opus, opus, operis, operi, opere*
(Plur.)	*opera, opera, opera, operum, operibus, operibus*
(Sing.)	*corpus, corpus, corpus, corporis, corpori, corpore*
(Plur.)	*corpora, corpora, corpora, corporum, corporibus, corporibus*
(Sing.)	*jus, jus, jus, juris, juri, jure*
(Plur.)	*jura, jura, jura, jurum, juribus, juribus*

Exercise 27

(a) The queen gives lands which she has in England to the lord
     quas accusative (antecedent *terras*; the subject is in the verb *habet*), plur., fem.

(b)   This is the meadow which has many cows
      quod nominative (subject of verb *habet*), sing., neut.
(c)   Edward gave to the church the meadows which he held in the manor
      que accusative (the subject is in the verb *tenebat*), plur., neuter
(d)   Robert is the farmer to whom I gave the land
      cui dative (of indirect object), sing., masc. (antecedent *agricola*)
(e)   The king gave lands to the lords whose knights fought bravely
      quorum genitive of possession, plur., masc. (antecedent *dominis*)
(f)   William is the lord whose lands lie in the parish
      cuius genitive, sing., masc. (antecedent *Willelmus*)
(g)   Ranulph holds two acres of which one acre lies next to John's land
      quarum genitive, plural, fem. (antecedent *acras*)
(h)   I Earl Ranulph give and by this charter have confirmed to Walter my son the
      meadow which I held in the parish
      quod accusative, direct object of *habebam*, sing., neuter
(i)   This is the charter by which I hold the land
      qua ablative (of means by which), sing., fem. (antecedent *carta*)

Exercise 28

(a)   I Richard of Bronston have given and by this my charter have confirmed to Henry
      of Winshill all the messuages which I held in the parish
      hac, mea, ablative, singular, feminine, agreeing with *carta*
      omnia accusative, plural, neuter, agreeing with *messuagia*
(b)   We John de Brailes and Agnes my wife have confirmed to Roger the chaplain all
      my lands with all meadows belonging to the same for the term of his life
      mea nominative, singular, feminine, agreeing with *uxor; meas* accusative, plural,
      feminine, agreeing with *terras*; *omnibus* ablative plural neuter agreeing with *pratis;*
      sue genitive, singular, feminine agreeing with *vite*
(c)   Likewise I leave to Michael, rector of the parish church 2s.6d.
      parochialis genitive, singular, feminine agreeing with *ecclesie*
(d)   The aforesaid John took from the lord all and singular the aforesaid premises for
      services owed according to the custom of the manor aforesaid
      Predictus nominative, singular, masculine agreeing with *Johannes; omnia, singula,*
      predicta accusative, plural, neuter agreeing with *premissa; debitis* (past participle
      used as an adjective) ablative, plural, feminine, agreeing with *serviciis; predicti,*
      genitive, singular, neuter, agreeing with *manerii*
(e)   And he gives to the lord for a fine at his entry 12d.
      suum accusative, singular, masculine, agreeing with *ingressum*

Exercise 29

(a)   Where is the road leading to the town?
      ducens nominative, singular, feminine, agreeing with *via* (nominative complement
      of *est*)
(b)   I see the road leading to the town
      ducentem accusative, singular, feminine, agreeing with *viam*
(c)   Nine acres of arable land lying in the aforesaid town are demised to the abbey
      iacentes nominative, plural, feminine, agreeing with *acre*

(d)   We John of Hopton and Matilda my wife have appointed Gilbert (our) attorney
      giving full power to the same
      dantes nominative, plural, masc., and fem. agreeing with *Johannes* and *Matilda*
(e)   Henry de Verdon gives to the abbey of Croxden one virgate of land with all
      meadows lying in his manor
      iacentibus abl., plur., neuter agreeing with *pratis*

Exercise 30
(a)   The queen gave to William the land called Horsehay
      vocatam accusative, singular, feminine agreeing with *terram*
(b)   The messuage called Hautassise lies in Bradeway
      vocatum nominative, singular, neuter agreeing with *messuagium*
(c)   By this indented charter we have confirmed a virgate of land to Ranulph
      indentata ablative, singular, feminine agreeing with *carta*
(d)   Andrew Paschal, gentleman, son of Andrew Paschal, knight, holds one messuage
      called Foxholes
      vocatum accusative, singular, neuter agreeing with *messuagium*
(e)   This is the final agreement made in the king's court
      facta nominative, singular, feminine agreeing with *concordia*
(f)   Francis Bartlett holds one acre of pasture lying in a field next to the lane called
      Le Hey
      iacentem (present part.) accusative, singular, feminine, agreeing with *acram; vocatam*
      accusative, singular, feminine agreeing with *venellam* (acc. after *iuxta*)
(g)   William Normansell surrenders into the hands of the lord two closes lying in the
      parish which he held by right of Elizabeth his wife
      iacentia accusative, plural, neuter agreeing with *clausa* (*clausum* is a variant of
      clausura more commonly found)

Exercise 31
(a)   Nicholas Bold and Robert Bydell, tithing-men, present Thomas Clerke and Henry
      Chatcull for default of appearance
(b)   Richard Messing obstructed the road leading to the church
(c)   To this court comes John Welles, Esquire, and surrenders into the hands of the
      lord one cottage lately in the tenure of Robert Turner
(d)   He gave to the church one tenement abutting on the north on the road called Le
      Flete
(e)   Edward Aston, knight, held of the lord by copy of court roll two meadows lying
      between the lands of John Wise and the royal highway
(f)   The jurors elect John Sale to the office of tithing-man. (He is) sworn
(g)   The same Radulph, villein, shall lift hay for one day a year
(h)   The frankpledges present that Isabella who was the wife of Thomas de Rideware
      and who owes appearance has not come therefore she is in mercy
(i)   Know all men about to see or about to hear the present writing that I, Henry, have
      given and by this my charter have confirmed to the prior and monks of Tutbury
      two cottages with appurtenances lying in the aforesaid town
(j)   John Bardell holds certain parcels of demesne lands and pays yearly 13s.4d.
(k)   When she had taken the oath (literally, the oath having been taken) the lord
      absolved her

Exercise 32

(a)   The jurors say that all is well
(b)   Richard remises all his right
(c)   Edward Aston has died and there falls due to the lord a bull in the name of heriot. (*taurus* is nominative as the subject of *accidit*)
(d)   We order for ourselves and our heirs that the aforesaid town shall be a free borough
(e)   The aforesaid lord grants a gild merchant to the borough

Exercise 33

claudo 'to close, enclose'; *tango* 'to touch, concern'; *mitto* 'to send'

Present	Imperfect	Future
claudo	*claudebam*	*claudam*
claudis	*claudebas*	*claudes*
claudit	*claudebat*	*claudet*
claudimus	*claudebamus*	*claudemus*
clauditis	*claudebatis*	*claudetis*
claudunt	*claudebant*	*claudent*
tango	*tangebam*	*tangam*
tangis	*tangebas*	*tanges*
tangit	*tangebat*	*tanget*
tangimus	*tangebamus*	*tangemus*
tangitis	*tangebatis*	*tangetis*
tangunt	*tangebant*	*tangent*
mitto	*mittebam*	*mittam*
mittis	*mittebas*	*mittes*
mittit	*mittebat*	*mittet*
mittimus	*mittebamus*	*mittemus*
mittitis	*mittebatis*	*mittetis*
mittunt	*mittebant*	*mittent*

Exercise 34

(a)   And on this the aforesaid John came into the same court and took from the lord the aforesaid croft to hold to him and his heirs
(b)   And we, the aforesaid Henry and the aforesaid Margaret, will warrant acquit and defend those lands against all men
(c)   Know all men that we, Henry of Denstone and Margaret my wife, have given to William Welles all the lands which we held in the manor of Alton.

Exercise 35

(a)   The lord took the lands
(b)   I, Richard, have remised all my right
(c)   We, William and Elizabeth, have affixed our seals

(d) Valentine brewed twice
(e) Robert will give to the lord 12d.
(f) Samuel Lathropp was admitted tenant and did fealty to the lord
(g) Richard Porter has died since the last court
(h) The jurors elected John Blunt (as) tithing-man for the year
(i) The said Radulph will pay 2s. annually to the lord
(j) Adam le Verdon demised, surrendered, and granted to Radulph de Hassal one burgage, with buildings, in the town of Ruthin

Exercise 36
(a) Know all men that I, William, have given to Elena, my daughter, one messuage
(b) Know present and future men that I, Stephen, have granted one hide of land to God and Saint Mary
(c) Be it known (that) we, John of Bronston and Elizabeth my wife, have confirmed to Humbert one acre of arable land lying in the manor of Tatenhill and abutting on the common highway

Exercise 37
(a) If he holds the houses let him pay the rent (NB two subjunctive verbs susceptible of slightly varying wording)
(b) It is ordered that Henry be distrained and that he should be at the next court
(c) May he rest in peace
(d) Be it known to all (who) shall hear or see these letters
(e) And it is ordered that no tenant shall permit any other tenant to live with him in (his) house
(f) Let it be known to all that I, Robert, have appointed Gilbert my attorney
(g) If it should happen that the said Elizabeth shall die (literally shall have died) without legitimate heirs the aforesaid lands shall remain to John

Exercise 38
(a) All the lands are taken into the hands of the lord
(b) The frankpledges present (that) Adam blocked the common highway and it is ordered that the bailiff should distrain him
(c) Margaret is in mercy for trespass by her geese in the lord's meadow but because she is poor the fine is remitted
(d) The plea between John Wryght and Simon de Hanbur(y) is adjourned (respited) to the next court

Exercise 39
(a) The messuage is (was) called Highlands
(b) The masters were (are) are licensed
(c) Godfrey and Radulph are (were) admitted tenants
(d) Elizabeth daughter of John Port was baptised
(e) The croft is held by services thence owed and accustomed
(f) Likewise I leave to Margaret my daughter and to the heirs of her own body legitimately begotten two burgages

Exercise 40

(a)   I have given a church to have and to hold to Phillip for eight shillings to be paid to me annually

(b)   The aforesaid Katherine has granted to John her father one messuage to he held for all his life

(c)   I, Radulph, am bound to Humbert Pole in ten pounds of good and legal money of England

(d)   And he gives at (his) entry 5 shillings to be paid at the feast of the Purification

(e)   It is decided that the said Nicholas and John may have a day for agreeing. (*habeant* is present subjunctive plural 3rd person after a verb of command)

Exercise 41

by this my writing (*hoc, meo* are ablative singular, neuter adjectives agreeing with *scripto*)

giving to the same (to him) full power (*eidem* is a dative singular pronoun, indirect object of the participle 'giving'; *plenam* is accusative singular feminine agreeing with *potestatem*)

by this my indented charter (*hac, mea, indentata* are ablative singular adjectives agreeing with *carta*)

to this court (*hac* is accusative singular adjective agreeing with *curiam*)

in that messuage (*illo* is an ablative neuter adjective agreeing with *messuagio*)

Elizabeth and Geoffrey and Henry their son (*eorum* is a genitive plural masculine adjective)

he said on his oath (*suum* is an accusative singular neuter adjective agreeing with *sacramentum*)

with all appurtenances belonging to the same (*omnibus* is an ablative plural feminine adjective agreeing with *pertinenciis*)

this is the final agreement (*hec* is a nominative feminine singular pronoun) *finalis* is a nominative, singular, feminine adjective agreeing with *concordia*

Exercise 42

(a)   Edward cannot demand any title in the meadow

(b)   Robert and his heirs cannot claim any right

(c)   Adam Hichen complains of Henry Bust in a plea of debt

(d)   Nicholas the Comber complains of John of Stapenhill in a plea of trespass

(e)   The divine offices are laudably observed

(f)   Geoffrey de Monte is charged that he destroyed the pasture of his neighbours with his cattle

(g)   Margaret de Lacy was summoned to reply to Alice wife of John Brown in a plea of defamation (*summonita* participle in perfect passive agrees with *Margareta; respondendum* is acc. gerund)

Exercise 43

(a)   Be it known to all by the present (writings)

(b)   They are allowed (literally 'it is allowed to them') to do this

(c)   It is necessary for him to come

(d) It is (was) found by the homage that William Michell (has) died since the last court
(e) The bailiff is ordered to seize the best animal of the same William for a heriot
(f) Be it known to all ...

Exercise 44

(a) It is lawful (for) Henry (or 'Henry is allowed') to occupy those lands without rent
(b) When he dies the lord shall seize the best (literally 'better') animal
(c) For making payment I bind myself and my heirs
(d) Walter, by the grace of God bishop of Lichfield, to (his) beloved son in Christ, Master Robert, his archdeacon, greeting
(e) Therefore they remain in mercy as appears above their names (literally 'heads')
(f) They seek a day for a verdict to be declared and it is granted to them (*dicendo* ablative singular neuter gerundive agreeing with *veredicto*)
(g) John Payne acknowledged that he holds freely by charter one messuage

Exercise 45

(a) Janet Barne daughter of William Barne curate of Chester was baptised on the first day of March in the aforesaid year (*curati* is genitive masculine singular in apposition to *Gulielmi*)
(b) Robert son of Henry (was) buried (*filius*)
(c) Agnes daughter of a harlot called Alice (was) baptised the seventh day of July 1590 (*filia*)
(d) George Lee took Miriam Shemmonds to wife the 14th day of November 1644
(e) Marriage between William Gilbert and Elizabeth Marshall (was) solemnised (on) 15th October
(f) John Elison (on) Sunday 4th August while he pastures sheep in the fields (was) struck by a soldier and wounded in the brain from which wound he lingered to the sixth day and then died and on the seventh day of the same month was buried and on the same day the aforesaid soldier was hanged

Exercise 46

(a) Let a marriage licence be granted between Henry Aldridge of the city of Lichfield, unmarried, 23 years and more old, and Mary Parker of the parish of Ashton on Trent in the county of Derby, single, 25 years old
(b) Let a licence be granted between Robert Smith, single, 24 years old, of the parish of Barton under Needwood, and Anne Homfreys, single, 22 years old, of the same parish

Exercise 47

Know all (men) by the presents that we, Robert Vernon of the parish of Hanbury and Thomas Vernon, yeoman, are held and firmly bound to the Reverend Lord and Father in Christ Richard by divine permission Bishop of Lichfield in sixty pounds of good and lawful money of Great Britain to be paid to the same Lord Bishop or to his certain attorney Executors or Administrators, for making which payment well and faithfully we bind ourselves and our Heirs by the presents. Sealed with our seals dated the 13 day of the month of October in the seventh year of the reign of our lord George by the grace of god of Great Britain France and Ireland King, defender of the faith, etc. and in the year of the lord 1720

Exercise 48

(a) Ranulph Hardinge reads prayers in Thursfield chapel without licence and teaches boys in the aforesaid chapel
(b) Richard Copland and Joan his wife are not living together and the judge warned him to live with his wife or to visit the house at least once weekly under penalty ...
(c) Richard Hassall and Anne Heath were presented for adultery. On which day he appeared and confessed to the accusation (which had been) made. Whereupon the judge enjoined penances on him on Sunday for two weeks
(d) Robert Betson's wife is not attending church. Let her be summoned anew
(e) The judge enjoined compurgation on him by the hand of four neighbours
(f) They appeared and the lord warned them to repair the church pavement before the feast of All Saints next
(g) Then after his penitence the judge enjoined on him penances on Sunday next after the reading of the second lesson

Exercise 49

(a) Lord William Beane, abbot, says that the house is free from all debt. The divine offices, silence and the essentials of religion are laudably observed. Suspicious access of women to the brethren is forbidden and the contrary. All other things are regulated in good order
(b) Brother Robert Busby, prior, pittancer and chamberlain ... (says) that the seculars singing in the choir during divine (services) come in without surplices. The brothers do not wear breeches. Brother Elkyn is a trouble-maker and tells secrets
(c) Brother Thomas Baker ... (says) that the monastery beer is too thin
(d) Brother William Edys, kitchener, is not present

Exercise 50

(a) Son of God have pity on me
(b) Pity me and save me because I have hoped in thee
(c) Pray for the soul of Sir Radulph formerly rector of this church (*Dominus* is here a courtesy title for a cleric, not 'Lord')
(d) Christ loved us and washed our sins from us in his blood
(e) Here lies Thomas ... who died,....
(f) Here lie the bodies of Lewis Bagot knight and of Anne his wife who died the 5th day of September ... on whose souls may God have mercy
(g) May their souls, by the grace of God, truly rest in peace

Exercise 51

Whosoever thou art who shall pass by
Stay, read, weep;
I am what thou wilt be, I was what thou art,
Pray for me, I entreat you

Exercise 52

(a) In the name of God, amen, on Thursday in the feast of Saint Petronilla the virgin in the year of the lord 1487, I, Lady Alice Lee, make my will in this wise. First I leave my soul to God the father almighty, to the Blessed Mary and to all the saints, and my body to be buried at the pleasure of my executors

(b) Likewise I leave to the preaching brothers of Newcastle 10s. to celebrate a trental of Saint Gregory for me and my husband

(c) Likewise I desire that my executors shall pay or shall cause to be paid all the debts that I owe

(d) Likewise I ordain and make Hugh Egerton and Radulph Delves, esquires, my true executors so that they may dispose of all my goods and debts not bequeathed to the honour of God and the benefit of my soul

(e) In testimony of which, I, John Soldus, vicar of Awdley have affixed my seal to this present will

Exercise 53

The above-written will was proved before the lord at Lambeth on the penultimate day of the month of November in the year of the lord abovesaid by the oath of William Wadham procurator and administration was committed to Radulph de Laye, executor, for well and faithfully administering before the feast of the purification of the blessed Virgin Mary next

Exercise 54

(a) Let administration of the goods of John Allen, deceased, lately while he lived, of the parish of Cheadull, be granted to Elizabeth Allen, widow, wife of the said deceased

(b) The said Elizabeth Allen was sworn before me, Thomas Hubbocke, deputy

(c) William Harvey of Hulme in the county of Cheshire and Elizabeth Allen of Cheadle aforesaid are bound

Exercise 55

(a) Court baron held at Barton on Thursday next after the feast of Saint Barnabas the apostle in the 27th year of the reign of Henry VIII by the grace of god king of England, France and Ireland

(b) Court baron at Alrewas held on the morrow of Saint Bartholomew in the 43rd year of the reign of king Henry son of king John

(c) Court of the view of frankpledge held there for the manor aforesaid on 10th day of October in the 8th year of the reign of our lady queen Anne

Exercise 56

(a) Robert (the) baker essoined himself by Richard (the) clerk of common suit of court 1st

(b) William Adam essoined himself by Hugh (the) hayward of the same 2nd

(c) William Docerill essoined himself for appearance by William Crocket 1st

(d) The jurors on their oath present the following persons owe suit to this court and have made default

Exercise 57
(a) William Wryght and Henry his brother drew blood from Hugh son of Walter
(b) The frankpledges present that Alana wife of Robert Cuge sold ale contrary to the assize
(c) The frankpledge of Branston presents that Henry the Cartwright brewed contrary to the assize
(d) Likewise they present that Richard Porter 2d. assaulted John Cartwright against the peace. Therefore he (is) in mercy
(e) The 12 jurors present that Hugh de Menill 6d. and Robert 6d. his son unjustly drew blood from Robert de Gresley. They (literally 'who') were attached and found John of Bursincot and John of Stapenhill pledges. Therefore etc.

Exercise 58
(a) John Kemster complains of Agnes de Ragleye in a plea of trespass
(b) William Charle plaintiff against Robert Laster in a plea of debt. Pledges for prosecuting (are) John Hobbeson and Adam his brother
(c) The inquiry between the family of Henry de Fold and Alice wife of William Orme concerning the raising of the hue-and-cry is adjourned until next Saturday
(d) Richard Rond appeared in court against Henry de Wylinton who has not come and (his) pledge defaulted therefore he is better distrained

Exercise 59
(a) To this court came John Bowyer and surrendered into the hands of the lord of the manor aforesaid two acres of arable land
(b) To this court came John Welles, esquire, and surrendered into the hands of the lord of the manor one cottage and one close thereto pertaining lately in the tenure of Robert Turner deceased. (*pertinens* is a present participle accusative singular neuter agreeing with *clausum; tenura* is ablative, singular, feminine following the preposition *in* and expressing place where something is)

Exercise 60
To this court came Henry Shipton of Longdon in his own person and in full court he surrendered into the hands of the lord of the manor aforesaid by the rod according to the custom of the manor aforesaid one rod of arable land (more or less) lying in Le Churchfield which rod of land is part of a certain messuage of the aforesaid Henry Shipton to the use and behoof of William Pott, his heirs and his assigns for ever. And on this into that court came William Pott and petitioned to be admitted tenant and gave to the lord for a fine at his entry three shillings and did fealty and was thereupon admitted tenant

Exercise 61
(a) Court held on Saturday before the feast of the nativity of John the Baptist in the 23rd year of the reign of King Edward III after the Conquest
(b) Thomas de Curbeye who held of the lord 1 messuage and one virgate of land has died and the lord has for heriot 1 ox of value 2 shillings
(c) Thomas Gyn who held of the lord 1 messuage and a half virgate of land has died and the lord has 1 heifer of value 17 pence
(d) Thomas le Creighton who held 1 messuage has died and the lord has for a heriot 1 cow of value 18d.

Exercise 62

(a) Geoffrey de Kingston holds 1 burgage formerly belonging to Alan (the) glover paying to the abbot 12d.

(b) Elena daughter of Walter (the) dyer holds a meadow called Skyrmere formerly belonging to her father and stretching as far as the new bridge, paying to the almoner 3s.

(c) New Street begins. Robert of Winshill holds 1 burgage upon which he has 2 messuages formerly belonging to William le Palmer of Winshull, paying to the sacrist 12d.

(d) Note that this burgage formerly belonged to Richard Quenyld (the) carpenter son of Roger a villein who married Agnes Bronemay who was the daughter of Richard del Fold who afterwards became a leper and withdrew to a leper house without an heir ...

(e) John son of John de Cloddeshale holds 3 burgages of which 2 formerly belonged to Richard le Webbe in exchange for one acre in Cuckoomeadow for which he pays nothing by reason of the exchange and he pays for the third to the abbot 12d.

Exercise 63

(a) Rental made and renewed by the oath of John Blounte and Arthur Meverell on 20th April in the 15th year of the reign of our lady queen Elizabeth

(b) John of London holds one cottage and one acre of land which used to pay annually 3s. 6d. now 2s.

(c) Rent of one messuage demised to the heirs of Edward Proudeholme at the will of the lord paying therefor annually 9s. 4d.

(d) Thomas Hyron and John Alporte hold certain parcels of demesne lands and pay annually 13s. 4d.

Exercise 64

(a) He (The same) must reap in autumn for one day with one man and on the second day with two men without food

(b) And each week of works up to the feast of Saint Peter in Chains he must work for three days howsoever the lord shall wish

(c) He must plough twice in winter and once in Lent

(d) He shall find one man for lifting hay for one whole day and he shall carry two cartloads of hay to the lord's barn and he must hoe for one day before the feast of the nativity of Saint John the Baptist

(e) And every year on the vigil of Saint Martin he must take his plough to the place where the lord's ploughs are ploughing and there he must plough one and half acres

Exercise 65

(Summary) Ralph lord of Grendon grants to John de Clynton, lord of Colleshull, the manor of Scheneston with all appurtenances and rights together with a third part of the dowry held by Isabella his mother in the manor, who is to pay him annually one rose on the Sunday following the feast of the nativity of St. John the Baptist. Witnesses Robert de Pipe, Henry Mauveysin, John de Herumville, knights, Robert de Barre, William de Tamhorn, William De Freeford, William Hary, Radulf de Pipe. Dated at

Scheneston on the Sunday following St. Valentine's Day, 24 Edward III (21 Feb. 1350)

Exercise 66

Know present and future men that I, William, son of Radulph of the mill have granted in free and pure alms to the prior and monks of Tutbury twelve acres of land in Merston in a piece of cultivated land which is called Apecroft which Radulph my father held by gift of the aforesaid prior and monks. And in order that this may be firm and valid I have strengthened the charter with the confirmation of my seal

Exercise 67

Know all (men) both present and future that I, Huctredus, son of Nicholas of Brocton, have remised, released and quitclaimed and by this my charter have confirmed to Robert vicar of Dovebridge eight acres of land in the district of Brocton and a half acre of meadow with appurtenances to have and to hold to Robert himself and assigns and their heirs paying annually in respect thereof to the lord prior of Tutbury and to the convent of the same place three shillings and three pence namely at the feast of Saint John the Baptist eighteen pence and at the feast of Saint Michael ten and eight pence and at the Purification of the blessed Mary 3 pence. And I, truly Huctredus, and my heirs will warrant the said land with messuage in the town of Brocton against all men. In testimony of which to this present writing I have affixed my seal. These (being) witnesses John Welles, Roger Turner and others

Exercise 68

Know present and future (men) that I, Robert de Harekin, have granted, released and quitclaimed to the prior and convent of Tutbury all right and claim which I had or was able to have in a croft which the said prior and convent bought from Gardino son of Richard without any reclaim by me or by my heirs. For this gift, grant and quitclaim moreover the prior and monks have given to me 20 shillings sterling

Exercise 69

(a) This indenture witnesses that I, Adam Banks, have let at farm to Elizabeth Miller one cottage lying next to the common highway, to have and to hold to her and to her heirs freely, quietly and in peace for ten years following, paying to me and my heirs or assigns two shillings at the four terms of the year in equal parts. And I, the aforesaid Adam Banks and my heirs will warrant, acquit and defend all that cottage to the aforesaid Elizabeth against all men. In testimony of which to these indented writings I have affixed my seal. These (being) witnesses ...

(b) And if it should happen that the aforesaid rent in whole or in part, shall be unpaid, let it be lawful to the aforesaid Adam, his heirs and assigns, to distrain in all the aforesaid tenement

(c) And if it should happen that the aforesaid rent in part or in whole at any term in arrears shall be unpaid let it be lawful for the aforesaid Adam to enter and occupy that tenement without objection

Exercise 70

To all the faithful of Christ to whom the present indented writing shall (have) come Hugh Jones of the city of London, mercer, (sends) greeting in the lord eternal ... Know that I, the aforesaid Hugh Jones for a certain sum of money paid to me by Thomas Powntes of Longdon in the county of Stafford, have sold, bargained, enfeoffed, granted and by this my present indented writing confirmed to the aforesaid Thomas Powntes those lands in Longdon called Churchelandes ... To have, hold and enjoy all and singular the premises with appurtenances to the aforesaid Thomas Powntes, his heirs and assigns for ever ... And I, truly, the aforesaid Hugh Jones and my heirs will warrant and for ever defend all and singular the premises to the aforesaid Thomas Powntes his heirs and assigns against me and my heirs for ever by the present (writings) ... In testimony of which I, the aforesaid Hugh Jones ... and Thomas Powntes ... to these indentures have affixed our seals alternately. Dated 20th day of September in the 24th year of the reign of our lady Elizabeth

Exercise 71

This is the final agreement made in the court of the Lady Queen at Westminster on the morrow of Holy Trinity in the 29th year of the reign of the lady Elizabeth by the grace of god of England, France and Ireland Queen, defender of the faith, from the Conquest, before Edward Anderson, Francis Wyndham, judges, and other faithful (subjects) of the lady queen then there present between Robert Baker, plaintiff, and William Mascall and Agnes his wife, deforciants, concerning ten acres of meadow with appurtenances in Denham whence a please of covenant was summoned between them in the same court, namely that the aforesaid William and Agnes acknowledged the aforesaid tenement with appurtenances to be the right of Robert Baker himself as that which the same Robert had by gift of the aforesaid William Mascall and Agnes and (which) they remised and quitclaimed from themselves, William and Agnes and their heirs, to the aforesaid Robert and his heirs for ever. And moreover the same William and Agnes have granted for themselves and the heirs of the same William, that they will warrant the aforesaid tenement to the aforesaid Robert Baker and his heirs against all (men) for ever. And for this acknowledgment, remise, quitclaim, warrant, fine and agreement the same Robert Baker gave to the aforesaid William Mascall and Agnes eighty pounds sterling.

Exercise 72

Henry by the grace of god king of England, lord of Ireland, and Duke of Aquitaine, to his archbishops, bishops, abbots, priors, earls, barons, judges, sheriffs, reeves, ministers and to all his bailiffs and faithful (subjects) Greeting. Know ye that we have granted and by this our charter have confirmed ... to the burgesses of Newcastle under Lyme that our town of Newcastle shall be a free borough and that the burgesses of the same town may have a gild merchant in the same borough with all liberties pertaining in such a gild ... and that they may go through all our land with all their merchandise buying and selling ... in peace, freely and quietly ... These (being) witnesses William de Ferrars ... Geoffrey Despenser ... and others. Dated by the hand of the venerable father, Ralph bishop of Chichester, our chancellor, at Feckenham, on the 18th day of September in the 19th year of our reign.

Exercise 73

Know ye that I have granted to my demesne men of Chester and their heirs that no one may buy or sell any sort of merchandise which shall come to the city of Chester by sea or by land other than themselves or their heirs or by their permission except at the fixed fairs in the nativity of Saint John the Baptist and in the feast of Saint Michael. Wherefore I wish that my aforesaid men and their heirs may have and hold the aforesaid liberty of me and of my heirs for ever freely, quietly, honourably and peaceably. And I forbid upon penalty of ten pounds to be taken for my use that anyone shall hinder or oppress them in the said liberty ...

Exercise 74

(a) *cu(m) om(n)ib(us) aliis*   with all other;
(b) *p(re)fatu(m) tenem(en)tum* the aforesaid tenement
(c) *ubiq(ue)* everywhere
(d) *imp(er)petuu(m)* in perpetuity, for ever
(e) *libe(re) quiete b(e)n(e) et in pace* freely, quietly, well and in peace
(f) *in cui(us) rei testimoniu(m)* in witness of which
(g) *hiis testib(us) Joh(ann)e Proudfoot tunc balli(v)o, Walt(er)o* these being witnesses John Proudfoot then bailiff, Walter (the) dyer

Exercise 75

(a) *Hug(o) le P(or)ter recup(er)avit in cur(ia) plena vj hop(pas) fr(ument)i (e)t j q(ua)rt(erium) aven(e) de Joh(anne) Karles ad solvend(um) in festo b(eat)i Mich(aelis) a(nn)o xxiiij° ad hoc fidel(ite)r solvend(um) invenit pleg(ios) Henricum de Ford (e)t Rad(ulphum) de Peck*
(b) *Ph(ilipus) Pistor debet ixs.vjd Ric(ardo) Meysey It(em) deb(et) iijs.vjd. Matheo de Lodelow. It(em) d(ebet) d(omi)no ijs.vjd. It(em) vjd. It(em) Martin(o) Parcar(o) vjs.vjd. It(em) xiiijd. Enoc(o) de Novo Castro—q(ua)r(e) adjudicat(us) est ad carcere(m) quousq(ue) solvit tot(um) vel inven(er)it pleg(ios). It(em) d(ebet) xxd. Hanik(o) quos solvit p(ro) pleg(io) eiusdem*
(c) *Elizabeth dei gr(ati)a Angl(ie) Franc(ie) (e)t Hib(er)nie Regina fidei defensor (e)tc. Om(n)ib(us) ad quos p(re)sentes l(it)ere n(ost)re p(er)ven(er)int Sal(u)t(e)m. Sciatis q(uo)d Rob(er)tus Donnington in cur(ia) n(ost)ra coram Justic(iariis) n(ost)ris apud Westm(onasterium) impli(ci)tavit Rob(er)tum Hammerton et Margeriam ux(ore)m ejus de (e)tc.*

Appendices

Nouns

Table of Case Endings

Case	1st Decl.	2nd Decl.		3rd Decl.				4th Decl.		5th Decl.
				consonant		-i				
				Singular						
	f.	**m.**	**n.**	**m.f.**	**n.**	**f.m.**	**n.**	**m.**	**n.**	**f.**
Nom.	a	us(er)	um	various		is, es	e,l,r	us	u	es
Voc.	a	e(er)	um	various		is, es	e,l,r	us	u	es
Acc.	am	um	um	em	var.	em,im	e,l,r	um	u	em
Gen.	e	i		is		is		us		ei(ei)
Dat.	e	o		i		i		ui(u)		ei(ei)
Abl.	a	o		e		i or e		u		e
				Plural						
Nom.	e	i	a	es	a	es	ia	us	ua	es
Voc.	e	i	a	es	a	es	is	us	ua	es
Acc.	as	os	a	es	a	es, is	ia	us	ua	es
Gen.	arum	orum		um		ium		ium		erum
Dat.	is	is		ibus		ibus		ibus		ebus
Abl.	is	is		ibus		ibus		ibus		ebus

Most nouns of 1st decl. are fem. A few are masc. by meaning.

Most nouns of 2nd decl. are masc. There are a few fem. plus those fem. by meaning and there are a very few neuter including *vulgus* 'crowd' which is sometimes found as masc.

The stems of 3rd decl. nouns end in a consonant or contain an *-i*. They are of mixed gender.

4th decl. nouns are of mixed gender.

Nouns of 5th decl. are nearly all fem. and most have no plural.

Adjectives

	Singular		
	M	**F**	**N**
Nom.	bonus	bona	bonum
Voc.	bone	bona	bonum
Acc.	bonum	bonam	bonum
Gen.	boni	bone	boni
Dat.	bono	bone	bono
Abl.	bono	bona	bono

	Sing.		**Plur.**	
	M.F.	**N.**	**M.F.**	**N.**
N.V.	felix	felix	felices	felicia
Acc.	felicem	felix	felices,-is	felicia
Gen.	felicis	felicis	felicium	felicium
Dat.Abl.	felici	felici	felicibus	felicibus

	Plural		
	M	**F**	**N**
Nom.	boni	bone	bona
Voc.	boni	bone	bona
Acc.	bonos	bonas	bona
Gen.	bonorum	bonarum	bonorum
Dat.	bonis	bonis	bonis
Abl.	bonis	bonis	bonis

	Sing.		**Plur.**	
	M.F.	**N.**	**M.F.**	**N.**
N.V.	ingens	ingens	ingentes	ingentia
Acc.	ingentem	ingens	ingentes,-is	ingentia
Gen.	ingentis		ingentium	
Dat.Abl.	ingentis		ingentibus	

Numerals

Numerals are adjectives, but only the words for one, two and three, and the hundreds from 200 to 900 decline and agree with nouns. Cardinal numbers answer the question 'How many?', ordinal numbers answer the question 'Which in order of number?'

Unus, 'one'

	Singular			**Plural**		
	m.	**f.**	**n.**	**m.**	**f.**	**n.**
Nom.	*unus*	*una*	*unum*	*uni*	*une*	*una*
Acc.	*unum*	*unam*	*unum*	*unos*	*unas*	*una*
Gen.	*unius*	*unius*	*unius*	*unorum*	*unarum*	*unorum*
Dat.	*uni*	*uni*	*uni*	*unis*	*unis*	*unis*
Abl.	*uno*	*una*	*uno*	*unis*	*unis*	*unis*

Ullus, nullus, solus, and *totus* decline like *unus*

Duo 'two'   *Tres* 'three'

	m.	**f.**	**n.**	**m. & f.**	**n.**
Nom.	*duo*	*due*	*duo*	*tres*	*tria*
Acc.	*duos,duo*	*duas*	*duo*	*tres*	*tria*
Gen.	*duorum*	*duarum*	*duorum*	*trium*	*trium*
Dat.	*duobus*	*duabus*	*duobus*	*tribus*	*tribus*
Abl.	*duobus*	*duabus*	*duobus*	*tribus*	*tribus*

Duum is sometimes found for *duorum, duarum*

Mille is generally an indeclinable adjective
Milia is a noun and is followed by a genitive

Ordinal numerals decline like *bonus*
   Numeral adverbs, e.g. *bis,* 'twice' and *ter* 'three times', answer the question 'How many times?'

Roman Numerals	Cardinals		Ordinals	
			Nominative	Ablative
I	unus -a -um		1st	primus, -a, um	primo (on the first)
II	duo, due, duo		2nd	secondus (alter)	secundo
III	tres, tria		3rd	tertius	tertio
IV, IIII	quattuor		4th	quartus	quarto
V	quinque		5th	quintus	quinto
VI	sex		6th	sextus	sexto
VII	septem		7th	septimus	septimo
VIII	octo		8th	octavus	octavo
IX, VIIII	novem		9th	nonus	nono
X	decem		10th	decimus	decimo
XI	undecim		11th	undecimus	undecimo
XII	duodecim		12th	duodecimus	duodecimo
XIII	tredecim		13th	tertius decimus	tertio decimo
XIV, XIIII	quattuordecim		14th	quartus decimus	quarto decimo
XV	quindecim		15th	quintus decimus	quinto decimo
XVI	sedecim		16th	sextus decimus	sexto decimo
XVII	septemdecim		17th	septimus decimus	septimo decimo
XVIII	duodeviginti		18th	duodevicesimus	duodevicesimo
XIX, XVIIII	undeviginti		19th	undevicesimus	undevicesimo
XX	viginti		20th	vicesimus	vicesimo
XXI	viginti unus, unus et viginti		21st	vicesimus primus, unus et vicesimus	vicesimo primo
XXII	viginti duo, duo et viginti		22nd	vicesimus secundus, alter et vicesimus	vicesimo secundo
XXIII	viginti tres		23rd	vicesimus tertius	vicesimo tertio
XXIV, XXIIII	viginti quattuor		24th	vicesimus quartus	vicesimo quarto
XXV	viginti quinque		25th	vicesimus quintus	vicesimo quinto
XXVI	viginti sex		26th	vicesimus sextus	vicesimo sexto
XXVII	viginti septem		27th	vicesimus septimus	vicesimo septimo
XXVIII	viginti octo, duodetriginta		28th	vicesimus octavus, duodetricesimus	vicesimo octavo
XXIX, XXVIIII	viginti novem, undetriginta		29th	vicesimus nonus, undetricesimus	vicesimo nono
XXX	triginta		30th	tricesimus	tricestimo
XXXI	triginta unus, unus et triginta		31st	tricesimus primus, unus et tricesimus	tricesimus primo
XL, XXXX	quadraginta		40th	quadragesimus	quadragesimo
L	quinquaginta		50th	quinquagesimus	quinquagesimo
LX	sexaginta		60th	sexagesimus	sexagesimo
LXX	septuaginta		70th	septuagesimus	septuagesimo
LXXX, XXC	octoginta		80th	octogesimus	octogesimo
LXXXX, XC	nonaginta		90th	nonagesimus	nonagesimo
C	(100) centum		100th	centesimus	centesimo
CI	(101) centum et unus		101st	centesimus (et) primus	centesimo primo
CL	(150) centum quinquaginta		150th	centesimus quinquagesimus	centesimo quinquagesimo
CC	(200) ducenti, -ae, -a		200th	ducentesimus	ducentesimo
CCC	(300) trecenti		300th	trecentesimus	trecentesimo
CD, CCCC	(400) quadringenti		400th	quadringentesimus	quadringentesimo
D	(500) quingenti		500th	quingentesimus	quingentesimo
DC	(600) sescenti		600th	sescentesimus	sescentesimo
DCC	(700) septingenti		700th	septingentesimus	septingentesimo
DCCC	(800) octingenti		800th	octingentesimus	octingentesimo
DCCC, CM	(900) nongenti		900th	nongentesimus	nongentesimo
M, CIↃ	(1000) mille		1000th	millesimus	millesimo

Declension of Pronouns

	(Personal)				**(Reflexive)**	
	I	**thou**	**we**	**you**		
Nom.	ego	tu	nos	vos	—	(no nom. case)
Acc.	me	te	nos	vos	se, sese	himself, herself, itself, themselves
Gen.	mei	tui	nostri	vestri	sui	of himself, etc.
			nostrum	vestrum		
Dat.	mihi	tibi	nobis	vobis	sibi	to himself
Abl.	me	te	nobis	vobis	se, sese	from himself, etc.

For the pers.pron. of 3rd pers. use *is, ea, id* 'he, she, it'
For the reflexive pron. of 1st and 2nd pers. use oblique cases of *ego* and *tu*

(Demonstrative)
hic this (near me), he, she, it

	Singular			**Plural**		
	m.	**f.**	**n.**	**m.**	**f.**	**n.**
Nom.	hic	hec	hoc	hi	he	hec
Acc.	hunc	hanc	hoc	hos	has	hec
Gen.	huius	huius	huius	horum	harum	horum
Dat.	huic	huic	huic	his	his	his
Abl.	hoc	hac	hoc	his	his	his

ille that (yonder), he, she, it

	m.	f.	n.	m.	f.	n.
Nom.	ille	illa	illud	illi	ille	illa
Acc.	illum	illam	illud	illos	illas	illa
Gen.	illius	illius	illius	illorum	illarum	illorum
Dat.	illi	illi	illi	illis	illis	illis
Abl.	illo	illa	illo	illis	illis	illis

Is that, he she, it

	m.	f.	n.	m.	f.	n.
Nom.	is	ea	id	ii	eae	ea
Acc.	eum	eam	id	eos	eas	ea
Gen.	eius	eius	eius	eorum	earum	eorum
Dat.	ei	ei	ei	eis, iis	eis, iis	eis, iis
Abl.	eo	ea	eo	eis, iis	eis, iis	eis, iis

iste that (near you) is declined like *ille*

(Definitive)

idem the same

| | **Singular** | | | **Plural** | | |
	m.	f.	n.	m.	f.	n.
Nom.	idem	eadem	idem	eidem	eaedem	eadem
Acc.	eundem	eandem	idem	eosdem	easdem	eadem
Gen.	eiusdem	eiusdem	eiusdem	eorundem	earundem	eorundem
Dat.	eidem	eidem	eidem	isdem or eisdem		
Abl.	eodem	eadem	eodem	isdem or eisdem		

(Intensive)

ipse self (he himself)

	m.	f.	n.	m.	f.	n.
Nom.	ipse	ipsa	ipsum	ipsi	ipse	ipsa
Acc.	ipsum	ipsam	ipsum	ipsos	ipsas	ipsa
Gen.	ipsius	ipsius	ipsius	ipsorum	ipsarum	ipsorum
Dat.	ipsi	ipsi	ipsi	ipsis	ipsis	ipsis
Abl.	ipso	ipsa	ipso	ipsis	ipsis	ipsis

(Relative)

qui who, which

	m.	f.	n.	m.	f.	n.
Nom.	qui	que	quod	qui	que	que
Acc.	quem	quam	quod	quos	quas	que
Gen.	cuius	cuius	cuius	quorum	quarum	quorum
Dat.	cui	cui	cui	quibus	quibus	quibus
Abl.	quo	qua	quo	quibus	quibus	quibus

(Interrogative)

quis, who? what?

Nom.	quis	quis	quid	In all other cases similar to Relative Pronoun
	qui	que	quod	
Acc.	quem	quam	quid	

(Indefinite)

quis anyone, anything

Nom.	quis	qua	quid	In all other cases similar to Relative Pronoun
	qui	qua	quod	except that *qua* or *que* can be used in neuter
Acc.	quem	quam	quid	nominative and accusative plural
	quem	quam	quod	

In declining compound pronouns such as *quidam* 'a certain person or thing' the suffix, in this instance *-dam* is unaltered and only the first element changes e.g. *quidam, quemdam, cuiusdam,* etc.

alius 'other', 'another' is both a pronoun and adjective, declining thus:

	Singular			Plural		
	m.	f.	n.	m.	f.	n.
Nom.	alius	alia	aliud	alii	alie	alia
Acc.	alium	aliam	aliud	alios	alias	alia
Gen.	alius	alius	alius	aliorum	aliarum	aliorum
Dat.	alii	alii	alii	aliis	aliis	aliis
Abl.	alio	alia	alio	aliis	aliis	aliis

to avoid confusion between the nominative and genitive singular forms *alterius* or *alienus* may be used for the latter

alter 'the other' (of two)

	Singular			Plural		
	m.	f.	n.	m.	f.	n.
Nom.	alter	altera	alterum	alteri	altere	altera
Acc.	alterum	alteram	alterum	alteros	alteras	altera
Gen.	alterius	alterius	alterius	alterorum	alterarum	alterorum
Dat.	alteri	alteri	alteri	alteris	alteris	alteris
Abl.	altero	altera	altero	alteris	alteris	alteris

The Conjugation of Verbs

Indicative, Active

sum—(I am)

Present		Future		Imperfect	
sum	I am	*ero*	I shall be,	*eram*	I was,
es	Thou art	*eris*	etc.	*eras*	etc.
est	He, She, it is	*erit*		*erat*	
sumus	We are	*erimis*		*eramus*	
estis	You are	*eritis*		*eratis*	
sunt	They are	*erunt*		*erant*	

Perfect		Future Perfect		Pluperfect	
fui	I have been,	*fuero*	I shall have	*fueram*	I had been,
fuisti	(or was)	*fueris*	been, etc.	*fueras*	etc.
fuit		*fuerit*		*fuerat*	
fuimus		*fuerimus*		*fueramus*	
fuistis		*fueristis*		*fueratis*	
fuerunt		*fuerint*		*fuerant*	

Subjunctives

Present	Perfect	Imperfect
sim	*fuerim*	*essem*
sis	*fueris*	*esses*
sit	*fuerit*	*esset*
simus	*fuerimus*	*essemus*
sitis	*fueritis*	*essetis*
sint	*fuerint*	*essent*

Pluperfect	Infinitives		Imperatives		
fuissem					
fuisses	*esse*	to be	*es, esto*	(sing.) be	
fuisset	*fuisse*	to have been	*este, estote*	(plur.) be	
fuissemus	*futurus esse*	to be about	*sunto*	let them be	
fuissetis	*fore*	to be			
fuissent					

Participles

Present	(none)	
Future	*futurus*	about to be

In the Pres., Subj. you may find *siem, sies, siet, sient,* also *fuam, fuas, fuat, fuant*.
In the Imperf. Subj. you may find *forem, fores, foret, forent*

Sum is not only a verb in its own right but is used as an auxiliary in the conjugation of other verbs, e.g. *obligatus sum* I am bound

Like *sum* are conjugated its compounds *absum* am absent, *adsum* am present

First Conjugation

voce, vocare, vocavi, vocatum (call, name)

Indicative, Active

Present	Future	Imperfect
voco	vocabo	vocabam
vocas	vocabis	vocabas
vocat	vocabit	vocabat
vocamus	vocabimus	vocabamus
vocatis	vocabitis	vocabatis
vocant	vocabunt	vocabant

Imperatives

Singular	Plural	
voca	vocate	'call'
vocato	vocatote*	
vocato*	vocanto*	'let him/them call'
		*mostly classical

Infinitives

Pres.	vocare
Fut.	vocaturus esse
Perf.	vocavisse

Perfect	Fut.Perf.	Pluperfect
vocavi	vocavero	vocaveram
vocavisti	vocaveris	vocaveras
vocavit	vocaverit	vocaverat
vocavimus	vocaverimus	vocaveramus
vocavistis	vocaveritis	vocaveratis
vocaverunt	vocaverint	vocaverant

Participles

Pres.	vocans
Fut.	vocaturus

Gerund vocandum

Subjunctives

Present	Perfect	Imperfect	Pluperfect
vocem	vocaverim	vocarem	vocavissem
voces	vocaveris	vocares	vocavisses
vocet	vocaverit	vocaret	vocavisset
vocemus	vocaverimus	vocaremus	vocavissemus
vocetis	vocaveritis	vocaretis	vocavissetis
vocent	vocaverint	vocarent	vocavissent

Indicative, Passive

Present	Future	Imperfect
vocar	vocabor	vocabar
vocaris	vocaberis(-re)	vocabarisi(-re)
vocatur	vocabitur	vocabtur
vocamur	vocabimur	vocabamur
vocamini	vocabimini	vocabamini
vocantur	vocabuntur	vocabantur

Imperatives

Singular	Plural	
vocare	vocamini	'be called'
vocator	vocantor	'let him/them be called'

Infinitives

Fut.	vocatum iri
Perf.	vocatus esse

Perfect	Fut.Pef.	Pluperfect
vocatus sum	vocatus ero	vocatus eram
vocatus es	vocatus eris	vocatus eras
vocatus est	vocatus erit	vocatus erat
vocati sumus	vocati erimus	vocati eramus
vocati estis	vocati eritis	vocati eratis
vocati sunt	vocati erunt	vocati erant

Particple

Perf.	vocatus

Gerundive

vocandus

Subjunctives

Present	Perfect	Imperfect	Pluperfect
vocer	vocatus sim	vocarer	vocatus essem
voceris(-re)	vocatus sis	vocareris(-re)	vocatus esses
vocetur	vocatus sit	vocaretur	vocatus esset
vocemur	vocati simus	vocaremur	vocati essemus
vocemini	vocati sitis	vocaremini	vocati essetis
vocentur	vocati sint	vocarentur	vocati essent

Second Conjugation

moneo, monere, monui, monitum (advise, warn)

Indicative, Active

Present	Future	Imperfect
moneo	*monebo*	*monebam*
mones	*monebis*	*monebas*
monet	*monebit*	*monebat*
monemus	*monebimus*	*monebamus*
monetis	*monebitis*	*monebatis*
monent	*monebunt*	*monebant*

Imperatives

Singular	Plural	
mone	*monete*	'advise'
moneto	*montetote**	'let him/them advise'
*moneto**	*monento**	(*mostly classical)

Infinitives

Pres.	*monere*
Fut.	*moniturus esse*
Perf.	*monuisse*

Perfect	Fut.Perfect	Pluperfect
monui	*monuero*	*monueram*
monuisti	*monueris*	*monueras*
monuit	*monuerit*	*monuerat*
monuimus	*monuerimus*	*monueramus*
monuistis	*monueritis*	*monueratis*
monuerunt	*monuerint*	*monuerant*

Participles

Pres.	*monens*
Fut.	*moniturus*

Gerund

monendum

Subjunctives

Present	Perfect	Imperfect	Pluperfect
moneam	*monuerim*	*monerem*	*monuissem*
moneas	*monueris*	*moneres*	*monuisses*
moneat	*monuerit*	*moneret*	*monuisset*
moneamus	*monuerimus*	*moneremus*	*monuissemus*
moneatis	*monueritis*	*moneretis*	*monuissetis*
moneant	*monuerint*	*monerent*	*monuissent*

Indicative, Passive

Present	Future	Imperfect
moneor	*monebor*	*monebar*
moneris	*moneberis(-re)*	*monebaris(-re)*
monetur	*monebitur*	*monebatur*
monemur	*monebimur*	*monebamur*
monemini	*monebimini*	*monebamini*
monentur	*monebuntur*	*monebantur*

Imperatives

Singular	Plural	
monere	*monemini*	'be advised'
monetor		'let him/them be
monetor	*monentur*	advised'

Infinitives

Pres.	*moneri*
Fut.	*monitum iri*
Perf.	*monitus esse*

Perfect	Fut.Perfect	Pluperfect
monitus sum	*monitus ero*	*monitus eram*
monitus es	*monitus eris*	*monitus eras*
monitus est	*monitus erit*	*monitus erat*
moniti sumus	*moniti erimus*	*moniti eramus*
moniti estis	*moniti eritis*	*moniti eratis*
moniti sunt	*moniti erunt*	*moniti erant*

Participle

Perf.	*monitus*

Gerundive

monendus

Subjunctives

Present	Perfect	Imperfect	Pluperfect
monear	*monitus sim*	*monerer*	*monitus essem*
monearis(-re)	*monitus sis*	*monereris(-re)*	*monitus esses*
moneatur	*monitus sit*	*moneretur*	*monitus esset*
moneamur	*moniti simus*	*moneremur*	*moniti essemus*
moneamini	*moniti sitis*	*moneremini*	*moniti essetis*
moneantur	*moniti sint*	*monerentur*	*moniti essent*

Third Conjugation
rego, regere, rexi, rectum (rule)

Indicative, Active

Present	Future	Imperfect	Singular	Plural	
rego	*regam*	*regebam*	*rege*	*regite*	'rule'
regis	*reges*	*regebas*	*regito*	*regitote**	'let him/them rule'
regit	*reget*	*regebat*	*regito**	*regunto**	(*mostly classical)
regimus	*regemus*	*regebamus*			
regitis	*regetis*	*regebatis*			
regunt	*regent*	*regebant*			

Imperatives Imperfect

Infinitives
Pres. *regere*
Fut. *recturus esse*
Perf. *rexisse*

Perfect	Fut.Perfect	Pluperfect	Participles	
rexi	*rexero*	*rexeram*	Pres.	*regens*
rexisti	*rexeris*	*rexeras*	Fut.	*recturus*
rexit	*rexerit*	*rexerat*		
reximus	*rexerimus*	*rexeramus*		
rexistis	*rexeritis*	*rexeratis*		
rexerunt	*rexerint*	*rexerant*		

Gerund
regendum

Subjunctives

Present	Perfect	Imperfect	Pluperfect
regam	*rexerim*	*regerem*	*rexissem*
regas	*rexeris*	*regeres*	*rexisses*
regat	*rexerit*	*regeret*	*rexisset*
regamus	*rexerimus*	*regeremus*	*rexissemus*
regatis	*rexeritis*	*regeretis*	*rexissetis*
regant	*rexerint*	*regerent*	*rexissent*

Indicative, Passive

Present	Future	Imperfect	Singular	Plural	
regor	*regar*	*regebar*	*regere*	*regimini*	'be ruled'
regeris	*regeris(-re)*	*regebaris(-re)*	*regitor*		
regitur	*regetur*	*regebatur*	*regitor*	*reguntor*	'let him/them be ruled'
regimur	*regemur*	*regebamur*			
regimini	*regemini*	*regebamini*			
reguntur	*regentur*	*regebantur*			

Imperatives Singular

Infinitives
Pres. *regi*
Fut. *rectum iri*
Perf. *rectus esse*

Perfect	Fut.Perfect	Pluperfect	Participle	
rectus sum	*rectus ero*	*rectus eram*	Perf.	*rectus*
rectus es	*rectus eris*	*rectus eras*		
rectus est	*rectus erit*	*rectus erat*		
recti sumus	*recti erimus*	*recti eramus*		
recti estis	*recti eritis*	*recti eratis*		
recti sunt	*recti erunt*	*recti erant*		

Gerundive
regendus

Subjunctives

Present	Perfect	Imperfect	Pluperfect
regar	*rectus sim*	*regerer*	*rectus essem*
regaris(-re)	*rectus sis*	*regereris(-re)*	*rectus esses*
regatur	*rectus sit*	*regeretur*	*rectus esset*
regamur	*recti simus*	*regeremur*	*recti essemus*
regamini	*recti sitis*	*regeremini*	*recti essetis*
regantur	*recti sint*	*regerentur*	*recti essent*

Fourth Conjugation
audio, audire, audivi, auditum (hear)

Indicative, Active

Present	Future	Imperfect	Imperatives		
			Singular	**Plural**	
audio	audiam	audiebam	audi	audite	'hear'
audis	audies	audiebas	audito*	auditote*	'Let him/them hear'
audit	audiet	audiebat	audito*	audiunto*	(*mostly classical)
audimus	audiemus	audiebamus			
auditis	audietis	audiebatis			
audiunt	audient	audiebant	**Infinitives**		
			Pres.	audire	
			Fut.	auditurus esse	
			Perf.	audisse or audivisse	

Perfect	Fut.Perfect	Pluperfect *	Participles	
audivi	audivero	audiveram	Pres.	audiens
audivisti **	audiveris	audiveras	Fut.	auditurus
audivit	audiverit	audiverat		
audivimus	audiverimus	audiveramus		
audivistis **	audiveritis	audiveratis	**Gerund**	
audiverunt *	audiverint	audiverant	audiendum	

Subjunctives

Present	Perfect *	Imperfect	Pluperfect **
audiam	audiverim	audirem	audivissem
audias	audiveris	audires	audivesses
audiat	audiverit	audiret	audivisset
audiamus	audiverimus	audiremus	audivissemus
audiatis	audiveritis	audiretis	audivissetis
audiant	audiverint	audirent	audivissent

Indicative, Passive

Present	Future	Imperfect	Imperatives		
			Singular	**Plural**	
audior	audiar	audiebar	audire	audimini	'be heard'
audiris	audieris(-re)	audiebaris(-re)	auditor	audiuntor	'let him/
auditur	audietur	audiebatur			them be heard'
audimur	audiemur	audiebamur	**Infinitives**		
audimini	audiemini	audiebamini	Pres.	audiri	
audiuntur	audientur	audiebantur	Fut.	auditum iri	
			Perf.	auditus esse	

Perfect	Fut.Perfect	Pluperfect	Participle	
auditus sum	auditus ero	auditus eram	Perf.	auditus
auditus es	auditus eris	auditus eras		
auditus est	auditus erit	auditus erat		
auditi sumus	auditi erimus	auditi eramus	**Gerundive**	
auditi estis	auditi eritis	auditi eratis	audiendus	
auditi sunt	auditi erunt	auditi erant		

Subjunctives

Present	Perfect	Imperfect	Pluperfect
audiar	auditus sim	audirer	auditus essem
audiaris(-re)	auditus sis	audireris(-re)	auditus esses
audiatur	auditus sit	audiretur	auditus esset
audiamur	auditi simus	audiremur	auditi essemus
audiamini	auditi sitis	audiremini	auditi essetis
audiantur	auditi sint	audirentur	auditi essent

*   The alternative form omits 'v': i.e., *audieram*
**   The alternative form omits 'vi': i.e., *audissem*

Mixed Conjugation

capio, capere, cepi, captum (take)

		ACTIVE VOICE		PASSIVE VOICE	
		INDICATIVE	**SUBJUNCTIVE**	**INDICATIVE**	**SUBJUNCTIVE**
Present		*capio* *capis* *capit* *capimus* *capitis* *capiunt*	*capiam* *capias* *capiat* *capiamus* *capiatis* *capiant*	*capior* *caperis, -re* *capitur* *capimur* *capimini* *capiuntur*	*capiar* *capiaris, -re* *capiatur* *capiamur* *capiamini* *capiantur*
Future		*capiam* *capies* *capiet* *capiemus* *capietis* *capient*		*capiar* *capieris, -re* *capietur* *capiemur* *capiemini* *capientur*	
Imperfect		*capiebam* *capiebas* *capiebat* *capiebamus* *capiebatis* *capiebant*	*caperem* *caperes* *caperet* *caperemus* *caperetis* *caperent*	*capiebar* *capiebaris, -re* *capiebatur* *capiebamur* *capiebamini* *capiebantur*	*caperer* *capereris, -re* *caperetur* *caperemur* *caperemini* *caperentur*
Perfect		*cepi* *cepisti* *cepit* *cepimus* *cepistis* *ceperunt*	*ceperim* *ceperis* *ceperit* *ceperimus* *ceperitis* *ceperint*	*captus sum* *captus es* *captus est* *capti sumus* *capti estis* *capti sunt*	*captus sim* *captus sis* *captus sit* *capti simus* *capti sitis* *capti sint*
Future Perfect		*cepero* *ceperis* *ceperit* *ceperimus* *ceperitis* *ceperint*		*captus ero* *captus eris* *captus erit* *capti erimus* *capti eritis* *capti erunt*	
Pluperfect		*ceperam* *ceperas* *ceperat* *ceperamus* *ceperatis* *ceperant*	*cepissem* *cepisses* *cepisset* *cepissemus* *cepissetis* *cepissent*	*captus eram* *captus eras* *captus erat* *capti eramus* *capti eratis* *capti erant*	*captus essem* *captus esses* *captus esset* *capti essemus* *capti essetis* *capti essent*
Imperative		*cape, capite* *capito*, capitote** *capito,* capiunto**	'take' 'let him/them take' *mostly classical		

Pres. Partic. *capiens* **Infin. Pres.** *capere* **Fut. Partic.** *capturus* **Infin. Fut.** *capturus esse* **Infin. Perf.** *cepisse* **Gerund** *capiendum*	**Participle** *captus* **Gerundive** *capiendus*

Verbs with present stem conjugated like *capio* include the compounds of this verb and *facio*, 'make', *fodio* 'dig', *morior* (depon.) 'die', and others. Forms derived from present stem sometimes take Fourth Conjugation endings.

Irregular Verbs

possum, posse, potui 'to be able', 'can'

ACTIVE VOICE		
	INDICATIVE	**SUBJUNCTIVES**
Present	*possum* *potes* *potest* *possumus* *potestis* *possunt*	*possim* *possis* *possit* *possimus* *possitis* *possint*
Future	*potero* *poteris* *poterit* *poterimus* *poteritis* *poterunt*	
Imperfect	*poteram* *poteras* *poterat* *poteramus* *poteratis* *poterant*	*possem* *posses* *posset* *possemus* *possetis* *possent*
Perfect	*potui* *potuisti* *potuit* *potuimus* *potuistis* *potuerunt*	*potuerim* *potueris* *potuerit* *potuerimis* *potueritis* *potuerint*
Fut. Perfect	*potuero* *potueris* *potuerit* *potuerimus* *potueritis* *potuerint*	
Pluperfect	*potueram* *potueras* *potuerat* *potueramus* *potueratis* *potuerant*	
Present Inf. *posse*		**Perfect Inf.** *potuisse*

potens 'powerful' is an adjective, not a participle

Glossary

The glossary provides translations of only those words and phrases used in this book. For other words readers should refer to the word-lists and dictionaries listed in the appendix.

NOUNS are given in the nominative case with the genitive ending also provided to show to which declension the noun belongs, followed by the letter indicating the gender. A hyphen is used to represent the stem when other case-endings are given, e.g. *regina, -e* (f.) 'queen', but where necessary for clarity or irregular endings the full genitive form is given, e.g. *caput, capitis* (n.) 'head'. Spellings are those found in the documents used, and there are often many possible variants. In medieval documents 'c' and 't' are usually indistinguishable and sometimes both are provided e.g. *inquisicio, inquisitio* 'inquiry'; 'u' and 'v' are often interchangeable; classical Latin had no 'j' but medieval scribes used both 'i' and 'j', e.g. *ius, jus* 'right'. Any necessary further explanation of a word with two or more meanings is given in brackets, e.g. *libra* 'pound' (money).

ADJECTIVES which decline like nouns of the 1st and 2nd declensions have their masculine, feminine and neuter endings indicated, e.g. *proximus, -a, -um* (adj.) 'next'. Adjectives which decline like nouns of the 3rd declension are shown with masculine/feminine and neuter forms, e.g. *omnis, -e* (adj.) 'all'.

NUMERAL ADJECTIVES are separately listed.

PRONOUNS are shown in their nominative singular masculine, feminine and neuter forms, and the type indicated e.g. *hic, hec, hoc* (dem. pron.) 'this' or 'he, she, it'.

VERBS are shown in two ways: regular verbs of the 1st and 2nd conjugations, which follow the models provided in the tables, are followed by the numbers (1) or (2); verbs of the 3rd and 4th conjugations have the stem represented by a hyphen and are followed by the numbers (3) or (4), e.g. *remitto, -ere, -isi, -issum* (3) 'to remise'. Four forms are shown (where they exist), 1st person present tense indicative active, infinitive, perfect, and supine, and from these all the tenses can be formed. Where there are irregularities the verbs are shown in full.

PREPOSITIONS are followed by an indication of the case which they take e.g. *cum* (prep. + abl.) 'with'.

If CONJUNCTIONS introduce a subordinate clause in the subjunctive mood this is indicated e.g. *cum* (conj. + subj.) 'since'.

Abbreviations

abl.	ablative	dep.	deponent	part.	participle
acc.	accusative	f.	feminine	pers.	personal
adj.	adjective	imper.	impersonal	plur.	plural
comp.	comparative	indec.	indeclinable	prep.	preposition
conj.	conjunction	int.	interrogative	pres.	present
dat.	dative	m.	masculine	rel.	relative
def.	definite	n.	neuter	subj.	subjunctive
dem.	demonstrative	num.	numeral		

A

a, ab (prep.+abl.) from
abbas, abbati (m.) abbot
abbatia, -e (f.) abbey
abbutto (1) to abbut on
aborsus, -us (m.) abortion, miscarriage or *abortus*
absolvo, -ere, -solvi, -solutum (3) to absolve
absque (pre.+abl.) without
ac (conj.) and also *atque*
accessus, -us (m.) access, entry
accido, -ere, accidi (3) to fall due
accipio, -ere, -cepi, -ceptum (3) take, receive
acer, acris (adj.) sharp
acquieto (1) to acquit, discharge
acra, -e (f.) acre
ad (prep.+acc.), at, for, to
Adam, Ade (m.) Adam
adjudico (1) to condemn
admitto, -ere, -misi, -missum (3) to admit
administracio, -ionis (f.) administration
administrator, -oris (m.) administrator
administro (1) to administer
admitto, -ere, -misi, -missum (3) to admit
adolescens, -tis (m.) young man/woman
adsum, adesse, adfui to be present
adulterinus, -a (adj.) adulterous
adulterium, -ii (n.) adultery
aes, aeris (n.) money
aes alienum debt
afferator, -oris (m.) affeerer, assessor
affraia, -e (f.) affray
Agneta, -e (f.) Agnes
agricola, -e (m.) farmer
Alana, -e (f.) Alana
Alanus, -i (m.) Alan
Alicia, -e (f.) Alice
alienus, -a, -um (adj.) belonging to another
alioquin (adv.) otherwise
aliquis, aliquod (pron.) any
alius, alia, aliud (pron. and adj.) other
alternatim (adv.) alternately, interchangeably
amercio (1) to fine
Anglia, -e (f.) England
anima, -e (f.) soul

Anna, -e (f.) Anne
annuatim (adv.) annually
annus, -i (m.) year
ante (prep.+acc.) before
apostolus, -i (f.) apostle
apparentia, -e (f.) appearance
appareo, -ere, -ui (2) to appear (in court)
appono, -ere, -posui, -itum (3) to affix
apud (prep.+acc.) at, near
aqua, -e (f.) water
Aquitania,-e (f.) Aquitaine
arabilis, -e (adj.) arable
archidiaconus, -l (m.) archdeacon
archiepiscopus,-i (m.) archbishop
aretro (adv.) in arrears
armiger,-eri (m.) esquire
aro (1) to plough
assarta, -e (f.) assart (forest clearing)
assignatus,-i (m.) (an) assign
assigno (1) to assign
assisa, -e (f.) assize
assisus, -a, -um (past part.) fixed
assumptio, -ionis (f.) Assumption, also *assumpcio*
attachio (1) to attach
attornatus, -i (m.) attorney
auca, -e (f.) goose
audio, audire, audivi, auditum (4) hear
Augusta, -a, -um (adj.) name relating to Augustus; *mensis Augusti* the month of August
aut (conj.) or
autem (conj.) however, moreover
autumpnus, -i (m.) autumn
avena, -e (f.) oats
averium, -i (n.) cattle, animal (mostly plural)

B

ballivus, -i (m.) bailiff
baptizarium, -i (n.) baptismal dues
baptizatus, -a (past part.) baptised
baptismata, -e (f.) (the) baptised
barganizo (1) to bargain
Barnabas, Barnabe (m.) Barnabas
baro, -onis (m.) baron, tenant-in-chief

curia baronis court baron
Bartholomeus, -i (m.) Bartholomew
bastardus, -a (adj.) bastard (also found as noun)
beatus, -a, -um (adj.) blessed
bene (adv.) well
bis (adv.) twice
bonus, -a, -um (adj.) good
bona,-orum (n.plur.) goods
borealiter (adv.) on the north
bos, bovis (m.) ox
bosca, -e (f.) a wood, also *boscum*
bracce, -arum (f.plur.) breeches
bracio (1) to brew, also *brasio*
breviter (adv.) briefly
Britannia, -e (f.) Britain
burgagium, -ii (n.) burgage
burgensis, -is (m.) burgess
burgus, -i (m.) borough

C

caelebs, -libis (adj.) unmarried
calumpnio (1) to challenge, charge
camerarius, -ii (m.) chamberlain
campus, -i (m.) field
cancellarius, -ii (m.) chancellor
canto (1) to sing
capella, -e (f.) chapel
capellanus, -i (m.) chaplain
capio, -ere, cepi, captum (3) to take
capitalis, -e (adj.) chief
carcer, -eris (m.) prison
carectata, -e (f.) cartload
cario (1) to carry
carpentarius, -ii (m.) carpenter
carta, -e (f.) charter
caruca, -e (f.) plough
celebro (1) to celebrate (Mass)
celum, -i (n.) the heavens
centum (ind.) hundred
cerebrum, -i (n.) brain
certus, -a, -um (adj.) certain
Cestria, -e (f.) Chester
chorus, -i (m.) choir (part of church)
Christus, -i (m.) Christ
cibum, -i (n.) food

Cicestrensis, -is (m.) Chichester
cirotecarius, -ii (m.) glover
cito (1) to cite, summon
citra (adv. and prep. + acc.) since
civis, -is (m.) citizen
civitas, -tatis (f.) city
clameum, -ei (n.) claim
clamo (1) to claim
claudo, -ere, clausi, clausum (3) to close, *diem clausit extremum* he died
clausum, -i (n.) close (enclosure)
clericus, -i (m.) clerk
cognosco, -ere, -gnovi, cognitum (3) to acknowledge
cohabito (1) to live together
collegium, -ii (n.) college
comes, itis (m.) earl
comitatus, -us (m.) county
committo, -ere, -misi,-missum (3) to commit to
communia, -e (f.) common (land)
communis, -e (adj.) common
compareo, -ere, -ui (2) to appear (at court)
comperio, -ire, comperi, compertum (4) to find, *compertum est* it is (was) found *comperta* (n.plur.) findings (at visitation)
compendium, -ii (n.) book (summary)
concedo, -ere, -cessi, -cessum (3) to grant
concessio, -ionis (f.) grant
concilium, -ii (n.) counsel, deliberation
concordia, -e (f.) agreement
concordor (1, depon.) to agree, to come to terms
condo, -ere, -didi, -ditum (3) to make (a will)
condono (1) to excuse
confirmacio, -ionis (f.) confirmation
confirmo (1) to confirm
confrater, -tris (m.) brother
coniungo, -ere, -iunxi, -iunctum (3) to marry
connubium, -ii (n.) marriage
conquerens, -tis (m.f.) plaintiff
conqueror, -queri, -questus sum (3, depon.) to complain
Conquestus, -us (m.) the (Norman) Conquest
considero (1) to give judgment

consideratum est it is (was) decided

constituo, -ere, -stitui, -stitutum (3) to appoint

consuetudo, -inis (f.) custom

consuetus, -a, -um (adj.) accustomed

contento (1) to pay, satisfy

contingo, -ere, -tigi, -tactum (3) to come to pass, to happen

contradicio, -ionis (f.) objection

contra (adv. and prep.+acc.) before, against, contrary

contraho, -trahere, -traxi, -tractum (3) to contract (matrimony)

convencio, -cionis (f.) agreement, covenant, also *conventio*

conventus, -us (m.) convent (religious house not just female)

conventualis, -e (adj.) conventual

copia, -e (f.) copy

copulo (1) to join

coquinarius, -ii (m.) kitchener

coram (adv. and prep.+acc.) in the presence of, before

corpus, -oris (n.) body

cotagium, -ii (n.) cottage

crastinum, -i (n.) the morrow
  in crastino (+gen.) on the morrow (of)

crimen, -inis (n.) accusation

croftum, -i (n.) croft

cultura, -e (f.) piece of cultivated land in open field

cum (prep.+abl.) with

cum (conj.) when, since (+subj.)

curatus, -i (m.) curate

curia, -e (f.) court

curtilagium, -ii (n.) curtilage, courtyard

D

dampnum,-i (n.) damages

datus, -a, -um (past part.) dated

de (prep.+abl.) of, concerning, from

debeo (2) to owe, to be obliged to (do something)

debitus, -a, -um (past part.) owed, due

debitum, -i (n.) debt

decedo, -ere, -cessi, -cessum (3) to die

decennarius, -i (m.) tithing-man

defalta, -e (f.) default

defamatio, -ionis (f.) defamation

defectus, -us (m.) default

defendens, -entis (m.f.) defendant

defendo, -ere, -di, -sum (3) to defend (uphold claim)

defensor, -oris (m.) defender

deforciator, -oris (m.) deforciant (illegal occupant)

defunctus, -a, -um (past part.) deceased

deinde (adv.) then, next

demanda, -e (f.) demand

denarius, -i (m.) penny

depono, -ere, -posui, -positum (3) to depose (state in evidence)

deputatus, -i (m.) deputy

destruo, -ere, -struxi, -structum (3) to destroy

despero (1) to despair of

Deus, -i (m.) God

dico, -ere, dixi, dictum (3) to say

dictus, -a, -um (adj.) (the) said

dies, diei (m.) day (f. when meaning 'appointed day')
  dies Dominical/Solis Sunday
  dies Jovis Thursday
  dies Lune Monday
  dies Martis Tuesday
  dies Mercurii Wednesday
  dies Sabbati Saturday
  dies Veneris Friday
  quo die on which day

dilectus, -a, -um (adj.) beloved

diligo, -ligere, -exi, -lectum (3) to love

dimidia, -e (f.) half

dimidius, -a, -um (adj.) half

dimitto, -ere, -misi, -missum (3) to demise

discordia, -e (f.) discord

dispono, -ere, -posui, -positum (3) to distribute

distringo, -ere, -nxi, -ctum (3) to distrain

divinus, -a, -um (adj.) divine
  divina officia divine services

do, dare, dedi, datum (1) to give

doceo (2) to teach

doctor, -oris (m.) doctor
domina, -e (f.) lady
dominicalis, -e (adj.) demesne
dominicus, -a, -um (adj.) demesne, of or
  for a lord
dominium, -ii (n.) lordship
dominus, -i (m.) lord, Sir, judge
domus, -us (f.) house
donatio, -ionis (f.) gift, presentation
donum, -i (n.) gift
dos, dotis (f.) dowry
duco, -ere, duxi, ductum (3) to lead
dum (conj.) while
duo, due, duo (num.adj.) two
duodecim (num.adj.) twelve
durus, -a, -um (adj.) hard
dux, ducis (m.) duke

E

e (see *ex*)
ecclesia, -e (f.) church
eciam or etiam (conj.) also
economus, -i (m.) churchwarden, also
  oeconomus
edificium, -ii (n.) building
edifico (1) to build
Edwardus, -i (m.) Edward
ego (pers.pron.) I
elemosina, -e (f.) alms
elemosinarius, -ii (m.) almoner
Elena, -e (f.) Ellen
eligo, -ere, -legi, -lectum (3) to elect
Elizabetha, -e (f.) Elizabeth
Emanuelis, -is (m.) Emmanuel
emo, emere, emi, emptum (3) to buy
Enocus, -i (m.) Enoch
eo, ire, ivi, itum (4) to go
episcopus, -i (m.) bishop
equalis, -e (adj.) equal
ere (see *aes*)
escambium, -ii (n.) exchange
eschaeta, -e (f.) escheat
esse (see *sum*)
essentialia, -ium (n.plur.) essential qualities
essonia, -e (f.) essoin
essonio (1) to essoin

et (conj.) and
  et ... et both ... and
ex (prep.+abl.) from, out of; also *e*
exactio, -ionis (f.) demand, tax, also *exaccio*
excipio, -ere, -cepi, ceptum (3) to except
executor, -oris (m.) executor
exigo, -ere, exegi, exactum (3) to demand
extendo, -ere, -tendi, -tentum (3) to extend
extra (adv.) without
extraho, -ere, -traxi, -tractum (3) to extract

F

faber, fabri (m.) smith
facile (adv.) easily
facio, -ere, feci, factum (3) to make, do
falso (adv.) falsely
familia, -e (f.) family
fateor, -eri, fassus sum (2 depon.) to confess
Februarius, -ii (m.) February
fenum, -i (n.) hay
feodum, -i (n.) fee (inheritable property)
feoffo (1) to enfeoff
festum, -i (n.) feast (festival)
fidelis, -e (adj.) faithful
fidelitas, -tatis (f.) fealty
fideliter (adv.) faithfully
fides, fidei (f.) faith
filia, -e (f.) daughter (dat. and abl. plur.
  filiabus)
filius, -ii (m.) son
finalis, -e (adj.) final
finis, -is (m.) fine
fio, fieri, factus sum (3 passive of *facio*) to
  be made
firma, -e (f.) rent
firmus, -a, -um (adj.) firm. lasting, valid
firmiter (adv.) firmly
flos, floris (m.) flower
fore (fut. infinitive of *esse*)
forisfactura, -e (f.) penalty
forma, -e (f.) form
fornicatio, -ionis (f.) fornication
fortiter (adv.) bravely
fossa, -e (f.) dike, embankment, ditch
Francia, -e (f.) France
franciplegius, -ii (m.) frankpledge

frater, fratris (m.) brother
frequento (1) to frequent
frumentum, -i (n.) wheat
futurus, -a, -um (adj. and fut. part.) about-to-be; *futuri* future (men)

G

Galfridus, -i (m.) Geoffrey
gardianus, -i (m.) churchwarden
Gardinus, -i (m.) Gardinus (proper name)
gaudeo, -eri, gavisus sum (2, semi-depon.) to enjoy
gemellus, -a, -um (adj.) twin
    gemini, -orum (m.plur.) twins
generosus, -i (m.) gentleman
gens, -tis (f.) people
genus, -eris (n.) kind, sort
Georgius, -ii (m.) George
Gilbertus, -i (m.) Gilbert
gilda, -e (f.) guild
gnotus, -a (adj.) illegitimate
gratia, -e (f.) favour, grace, also *gracia*
gratum, -i (n.) consent
gravo (1) to oppress
Gregorius, -ii (m.) Gregory
Gulielmus, -i (m.) William

H

habeo, -ere, habui, habitum (2) to have
habendum et tenendum to have and to hold
hebdomadatim (adv.) weekly
Henricus, -i (m.) Henry
herbagium, -ii (n.) pasture
hercia, -e (f.) harrow
hercio (1) to harrow
hereditarius, -a, -um (adj.) hereditary
heres, -edis (m.f.) heir
heriettum, -i (n.) heriot
Hibernia, -e (f.) Ireland
hic, hec, hoc (pron.and adj.) here, this
hida, -e (f.) hide
homagium, -ii (n.) homage
homo, hominis (m.) man
honor, -oris (m.) honour
honorifice (adv.) honourably
hoppa, -e (f.) hopper

Huctredus, -i (m.) Huctredus (proper name)
Hugo, -onis (m.) Hugh
huiusmodi (adj. ind.) of this kind
Humbertus, -i (m.) Humbert
humilitatio, -onis (f.) repentance
hutesium, -ii (n.) hue-and-cry

I

iacens, -entis (pres.part.) lying
iaceo, -ere, iacui, iacitum (2) to lie, be situated also *jaceo*
ibi (adv.) there
ibidem (adv.) in the same place, there
idem, eadem, idem (def.pron.) the same
ideo (adv.) therefore
ignotus, -a, -um (adv.) unknown
ille, illa, illud (pron. and adj.) that, he, she, it
illegitimus, -a (adj.) illegitimate
impedio (4) to hinder
imperpetuum (adv.) for ever, in perpetuity, also *inperpetuum*
implicito (1) to implead (charge)
imprimis (adv.) first, firstly, also *inprimis*
in (prep.+acc. or abl.) in
incedo, -ere, -cessi, -cessum (3) to come in
incipio, -ere, -cepi, -ceptum (3) to begin
inde (adv.) thence, in respect thereof, then
indentatus, -a, -um (adj.) indented
indentura, -e (f.) indenture
infra (adv.) within, below
ingredior, -gredi, -gressus sum (3 dep.) to enter
ingressus, -us (m.) entry
iniungo, -ere, -iunxi, -iunctum (3) to impose, enjoin
iniuste (adv.) unjustly
inquisitio, -ionis (f.) inquiry, also *inquisicio*
insolutus, -a, -um (past part) unpaid
insula, -e (f.) island
integre (adv.) wholly, completely
inter (adv.and prep.+acc.) between
invenio, -ire, -veni, -ventum (4) to find, provide
ipse, ipsa, ipsum (pron. and adj.) self, he himself, she herself

Isabella, -e (f.) Isabel
iste, ista, istud (dem, pron. and adj.) this
item (adv.) likewise
ius, iuris (n.) right, form of law, also *jus*
iuxta (prep.+acc.) next to, adjoining, also *juxta*

J

Janeta, -e (f.) Janet
Januarius, -i (m.) January
Johannes, -is (m.) John
Julia, -e (f.) Julia
Juliana, -e (f.) Juliana
Julius, -ii (m.) July
jungo, -ere, junxi, junctum (3) to join
Junius, -ii (m.) June
juramentum, -i (n.) oath
jurator, -oris (m.) juror
juro (1) to swear
jus, juris (n.) right, law
justiciarius, -ii (m.) justice
juvenca, -e (f.) heifer
juxta (adv. and prep.+acc.) near to, according to

L

laboro (1) to work
langueo (2) to linger
laudabiliter (adv.) laudably
lavo (1) to wash
lectio, -ionis (f.) reading
lectura, -e (f.) lesson
legalis, -e (adj.) lawful
legitime (adv.) lawfully
legitimus, -a, -um (adj.) legal, lawful
lego (1) to leave (bequeath)
lego, -ere, legi, lectum (3) to read
Leonardus, -i (m.) Leonard
leprosus, -i (m.) leper
levo (1) to raise
lex, legis (f.) law
liber, libera, liberum (adj.) free
libere (adv.) freely
libertas, -tatis (f.) liberty (franchise)
libra, -e (f.) pound (money)
licencia, -e (f.) licence

licencio (1) to license
licet (imper.verb +dat.) it is allowed, lawful
littera, -e (f.) letter
locus, -i (m.) place
luna, -e (f.) moon

M

magister, magistri (m.) master
magnus, -a, -um (adj.) great
maneo, -ere, mansi, mansum (2) to remain
manerium, -ii (n.) manor
manus, -us (f.) hand
mare, -is (n.) sea
Margeria, -e (f.) Margery
Maria, -e (f.) Mary
marito (1) to marry
maritus, -i (m.) husband
Martinus, -i (m.) Martin
martir, -iris (m.) martyr
Martius, -ii (m.) March
mater, matris (f.) mother
Matilda, -e (f.) Matilda
matrimonium, -i (n.) marriage
matrimonialis, -e (adj.) matrimonial
Mattheus, -i (m.) Matthew
medietas, -tatis (f.) half
melior, melius (comp.adj. and adv.) better, best
memorandus, -a, -um (gerundive from *memoro*) to be remembered
memoro (1) to call to mind
mensis, -is (m.) month
mercandisa, -e (f.) merchandise
mercator, -oris (m.) merchant
mercer (English) rnercer
mercimonium, -ii (n.) merchandise
meretrix, -icis (f.) harlot
meridies, -iei (m.) noon
messor, -oris (m.) hayward
messuagium, -ii (n.) messuage
meto, -ere, messui, messum (3) to reap
meus, -a, -um (adj.) my
Michaelis, -is (m.) Michael
michi (dat. pers. pron.) to me (also *mihi*)
miles, militis (m.) knight (also found as classical 'soldier')

mille (indeclinable) thousand
minister, -ri (m.) officer, minister
minus (adv.) smaller
  ad minus at least
misereor (2 depon.+gen.) to pity
misericordia, -e (f.) mercy, amercement
mitto, -ere, misi, missum (3) to send
modo (adv.) now
modus, -ii (m.) manner
moereo (2) to grieve
molendinum, -i (n.) mill
monachus, -i (m.) monk
monasterium, -ii (n.) monastery
moneo (2) to warn
moneta, -e (f.) money
mora, -e (f.) moor
mors, mortis (f.) death
mortuus, -a, -um (adj.) dead
moveo, -ere, movi, motum (2) to move
mulier, -ieris (f.) woman
multus, -a, -um (adj.) many
munimen, -inis (n.) strengthening

N

nativitas, -itatis (f.) birth
nativus, -i (m.) villein
natus, -a, -um (past part.) born
ne (conj.+subj.) that ... not (lest)
nec (conj.) and not, nor (also *neque*)
nescio, -ire, -scivi, -scitum (4) not to know
nichil (indeclinable) nothing, also *nihil*
Nicholaus, -i (m.) Nicholas
nimis (adv.) too much
nisi (conj.) except
nomen, nominis (n.) name
non (adv.) not
nonus, -a, -um (num.adj. ordinal of *novem*) ninth
nos (pron.) we
nosco, -ere, novi, notum (3) to get to know
  notum sit be it known
noster, -tra, -trum (possessive pron. used as adj.) our
nothus, -a (adj.) illegitimate
November, -ris (m.) November
Novum, -i Castrum, -i (n.) Newcastle

novus, -a, -um (adj.) new
  de novo anew
nubo, -ere, nupsi, nuptum (3) to marry
  nomina nuptorum the names of the married
nullus, -a, -um (pron.adj.) none
nunc (adv.) now
nundine, -arum (only in f.plur.) fair
nuper (adv.) lately
nuptie, -iarum (f.plur.) marriage, nuptials

O

obeo, -ire, -ii, obitum (4) to die
obiecto (1) to charge (accuse)
obligo (1) to bind (secure on a sum of money)
observo (1) to observe
obstupo (1) to stop up
obtineo, -ere, -tinui, -tentum (2) to obtain
occupo (1) to seize
oeconomus, -i (m.) churchwarden, also *economus*
officium, -ii (n.) office
olim (adv.) formerly
omnis, -e (adj.) all
  omnium sanctorum festivitas feast of All Saints
omnipotens, -entis (adj.) almighty
operabilis, -is (adj.) working
operor (1 dep.) to work
oportet, oportere, oportuit (imp. verb +dat.) it behoves
oppono, -ere, -posui, -positum (3) to oppose (appear in court)
optime (adv.) best
opus, operis (n.) work, use
  ad opus et usum to the use and behoof
ordino (1) to order, appoint
ordo, -inis (m.) order, arrangement
oro (1) to pray
orreum, -i (n.) granary (also *horreum*)
ovis, -is (f.) sheep

P

pacifice (adv.) peacefully
pannagium, -ii (n.) pannage

parcarius, -ii (m.) parker
parcella, -e (f.) parcel, part
parcus, -i (m.) park
parens, -tis (m.f.) parent
parochia, -e (f.) parish
parochialis, -e (adj.) parochial
pars, partis (f.) part
parsona, -e (generally f. though m. in meaning) parson
pasco, -ere, pavi, pastum (3) to pasture
pastura, -e (f.) pasture
pateo, -ere, patui (2) to be manifest, clear
    pateat universis (pres.subj.) let it be known to all
pater, -ris (m.) father
pauper, -eris (adj.) poor
pavimentum, -i (n.) pavement
pax, pacis (f.) peace
peccatum, -i (n.) sin
pecunia, -e (f.) money
pena, -e (f.) penalty
penitencia, -e (f.) penance
penultimus, -a, -um (adj.) penultimate
per (prep.+acc.) through, by
percipio, -ere, -cussi, -cussum (3) to seize
percutio, -ere, -cussi, -cussum (3) to strike
peregrinus, -a (m.f.) tramp, vagrant, as adj. wandering
perlego, -legere, -legi, -lectum (3) to read through
permaneo, -ere, -mansi, -mansum (2) to endure
permissio, -ionis (f.) permission
permitto, -ere, -misi, -missum (3) to permit
persona, -e (f.) person also parson
pertinencia, -e (f.) appurtenances, also *pertinentia*
pertineo, -ere, -tinui (2) to belong to
    pertinens, -entis (pres.part.) pertaining, belonging
pervenio, -ire, -veni, -ventum (4) to come to, arrive at
peto, -ere, petivi, -itum (3) to petition
Petronilla, -e (f.) Petronilla
Petrus, -i (m.) Peter
Philippus, -i (m.) Philip

pietanciarius, -i (m.) pittancer
piscaria, -e (f.) fishing (rights)
pistor, -oris (m.) baker
placitum, -i (n.) plea (also pleasure)
plegius, -i (m.) pledge
plenius (comp. adv.) more fully
plenus, -a, -um (adj.) full
ploro (1) to weep
plus, pluris (adj.) more
pono, -ere, posui, positum (3) to place
    p- in respectu to adjourn, respite
populus, -i (m.) people
pons, pontis (m.) bridge
porcus, -i (m.) pig
portarius, -i (m.) porter
portio, -ionis (f.) part
possideo, -ere, -sedi, -sessum (2) to occupy, possess
possum, posse, potui to be able
post (adv. and prep.+acc.) after
postea (adv.) afterwards
potestas, -tatis (f.) power
potus, -us (m.) beer, drink
pratum, -i (n.) meadow
precipio, -ere, -cepi, -ceptum (3) to order, command
precor, -ari (1 dep.) to pray
predicator, -oris (m.) preacher
predictus, -a, -um (adj. and past part.) aforesaid
prefatus, -a, -um (adj.) aforesaid
premissa, -orum (n.plur.) premises
prepositus, -i (m.) reeve
presens, -entis (adj.) present
    presentes (f.plur.) letters, deed
presento (1) to present (make presentment)
presto, -are, prestiti, prestitum (1) to take, show, profess
    presto iuramentum to take an oath
preterea (adv.) moreover
pretium, -i (n.) price
prex, precis (f.) prayer usually plur. *preces*
primus, -a, -um (adj.) first
prior, -oris (m.) prior
prius (adv.) previously
pro (prep. and adv.) for

probo (1) to prove (a will)

probus, -a, -um (adj.) honest

procreatus, -a, -um (past part.) begotten

procurator, -oris (m.) proctor

proficuum, -i (n.) profit

prohibeo, -ere, -ui, -itum (2) to prohibit

propicior (1 dep.+dat.) to have mercy on also *propitior*

proprius, -a, -um (adj.) (one's) own

prosequor, -sequi, -secutus sum (3 dep.) to prosecute

prout (adv.) according as

proviso quod (+subj.) provided that

proxime (adv.) next

proximus, -a, -um (adj.) next

puella, -e (f.) girl

puer, -eri (m.) boy

pugno (1) to fight

purgatio, -ionis (f.) purgation

Purificatio,-ionis   (f.)   Purification (churching)

purus, -a, -um (adj.) pure

Q

Quadragesima, -e (f.) Lent

qualitercumque (adv.) in whatsoever manner

quando (adv. and conj.) when

quare (conj.) wherefore

quartus, -a, -um (adj.) fourth

querela, -e (f.) suit (legal)

querens, -entis (m.f.) plaintiff

queror, queri, questus sum (3 dep.) to complain

quia (conj.) because

qui, que, quod (rel.pron.) who, which

quicumque, quecumque, quodcumque (pron.) whatsoever

quidam, quedam, quodam (pron. used adjectivally) a certain

quiesco, -escere, -evi, -etum (3) to rest

quietaclamantia, -e (f.) quitclaim

quiete (adv.) quietly

quietumclamo (1) to quitclaim

quilibet, quelibet, quodlibet (pron.) each, any

quinque (num.adj.) five

quintus, -a, -um (adj.) fifth

quis, quis, quid (interr.pron.) who? which? what?

quisquis, quisquis, quicquid (pron.) whosoever, whatsoever

quod (conj.) that

quondam (adv.) formerly

quoque modo in whatever way

quousque (adv.) until

R

racio, -ionis (f.) reason also *ratio*

Radulphus, -i (m.) Radulph (Ralph)

Ranulphus, -i (m.) Ranulph

ratus, -a, -um (adj.) valid, right

recedo, -ere, -cessi, -cessum (3) to withdraw

reclamatio, -ionis (f.) reclaim, counter-claim

recognitio, -ionis (f.) acknowledgment

recognosco, -ere, -gnovi, -gnitum (3) to acknowledge

rector, -oris (m.) rector

recupero (1) to recover

redditus, -us (m.) rent

reddo, -ere, -didi, -ditum (3) to pay, return

regina, -e (f.) queen

regius, -a, -um (adj.) royal

regnum, -i (n.) reign

rego, -ere, rexi, rectum (3) rule

relaxo (1) to release

relevium, -ii (n.) relief (feudal due)

religio, -onis (f.) religion

remaneo, -ere, remansi (2) to remain (in hands of another)

remissio, -ionis (f.) remission, written grant

remitto, -ere, -misi, -missum (3) to remise

renatus, -a, -um (adj.) reborn (baptised)

renovo (1) to renew

rentale, -is (n.) rental

reparo (1) to repair

requiesco, -ere, -evi, -etum (3) to rest

res, rei (f.) thing, matter

respectus, -us (m.) postponement, respite

respondeo, -ere, -spondi, -sponsum (2) to reply

retenementum, -i (n.) reservation

reverendus, -a, -um (adj.) reverend

revelator, -oris (m.) revealer

rex, regis (m.) king
Ricardus, -i (m.) Richard
Robertus, -i (m.) Robert
roboro (1) to strengthen
roda, -e (f.) rod (measure of land)
Rogerus, -i (m.) Roger
rogo (1) to ask
Roma, -e (f.) Rome
ropa, -e (f.) rope
rosa, -e (f.) rose
rotulus, -i (m.) roll (court roll)

S

Sabbatum, -i (n.) Saturday (not Sunday)
    die Sabbati on Saturday
sacramentum, -i (n.) oath also *sacrum*
sacrista, -e (f.) sacrist
saisio (1) to seize also *seiso* and *seisio*
salus, -utis (f.) greeting, salvation
salvo (1) to save
sanctus, -a, -um (adj.) holy, saint
sanguis, sanguinis (m.) blood
sarclio (1) to hoe
scilicet (adv.) namely
scio, scire, scivi, scitum (4) to know
scorta, -e (f.) prostitute
scriptum, -i (n.) writing, deed
secta, -e (f.) suit (of court)
secularis, -e (adj.) secular (also used as
    noun)
secum (adv.) with him
secundum (adv. and prep.+acc.) according
    to
secundus, -a, -um (adj.) second
sed (conj.) but
sedeo, -ere, sedi, sessum (2) to sit
semel (adv.) once
seminator, -oris (m.) sower
semita, -e (f.) lane
semper (adv.) always
sempiternus, -a, -um (adj.) everlasting
senescallus, -i (m.) steward
sepa, -e (f.) onion also *cepa*
sepelio, -pelire, -pelivi and *-pelli, -pultum*
    (4) to bury
September, -bris (f.) September

septimana, -e (f.) week
sepultus, -a, -um (past part.) buried
sequens, -entis (pres.part.) following
sequor, sequi, secutus sum (3 dep.) to follow
servicium, -ii (n.) service
servisia, -e (f.) ale also *cervisia*
servus, -i (m.) serf, villein
Sewinus, -i (m.) Sewinus (proper name)
shopa, -e (f.) shop, workshop
si (conj.) if
sibi (dat. of reflexive pron. *se*) to himself
sigillo (1) to seal
sigillum, -i (n.) seal
silentium, ii (n.) silence
Simo, Simonis (m.) Simon
sine (prep.+abl.) without
singuli, -e, -a (plur.adj.) each, every single
    one
sive (conj.) whether
socius, -ii (m.) fellow (of college)
solemnizo (1) to solemnise
soleo, -ere, solitus sum (2 semi-dep.) to be
    accustomed
solidus, -i (m.) shilling
solucio, -ionis (f.) payment
solutus, -a (adj.) single
solutus, -a, -um (past part.) paid
solvo, -ere, solvi, solutum (3) to pay
specto (1) to belong to
spero (1) to hope
sponsalia, -ium (n.plur.) espousal
spurius, -a (adj.) illegitimate also *spuriosus*
stabilis, -e (adj.) stable, valid
Staffordia, -e (f.) Stafford
stagnum, -i (n.) pond
Stephanus, -i (m.) Stephen
sterlingus, -i (m.) silver penny
    sterlingorum (gen.plur.) of sterling
sto, stare, steti, statum (1) to stand, stop
sub (prep.+ acc. and abl.) under
subter (adv. and prep.+acc. and abl.) below,
    under, also *subtus*
summa, -e (f.) sum
summoneo (2) to summon
super (adv. and prep.+acc. and abl.) above,
    on

superpellicus, -i (m.) surplice

supra (adv. and prep.+acc.) above

supradictus, -a, -um (adj.) above-mentioned

suprascriptus, -a, -um (past part.) above-written

sursumreddo, -ere, -reddidi, -redditum (3) to surrender

suspectus, -a, -um (part.) suspicious

suspendo, -ere, -di, -sum (3) to hang

suus, -a, -um (adj.) his, her, its

T

tam (adv.) so, so much, as
   tam ... quam both ... and

tango, -ere, tetigi, tactum (3) to concern

tannator, -oris (m.) tanner

taurus, -i (m.) bull

tempus, -oris (n.) time

tenementum, -i (n.) tenement

tenens, -entis (m.f.) tenant

tenentiarius, -i (m.) tenant

teneo, -ere, tenui, tentum (2) to hold

tenuis, -e (adj.) thin

tenura, -e (f.) tenure

tercius, -a, -um (adj.) third also *tertius*

terminus, -i (m.) term

terra, -e (f.) land

territorium, -ii (n.) district, territory

testamentum, -i (n.) will, testament

testimonium, -ii (n.) witness, testimony

testis, -is (m.f.) witness

testor (1 dep.) to witness

tinctor, -oris (m.) dyer

titulus, -i (m.) title, claim

totus, -a, -um (adj.) the whole, all

trado, -ere, tradidi, traditum (3) to leave, demise, lease

traho, -ere, traxi, tractum (3) to draw

transacto (1) to transact

transeo, -ire, -ii, -itum , (2) to pass by

transgressio, -ionis (f.) trespass

trentale, -is (n.) office of 30 masses

Trinitas, -atis (f.) Trinity

tristis, -e (adj.) sad

tunc (adv.) then

U

ubi (adv.) where

ubique (adv.) everywhere

ullus, -a, -um (pron. and adj.) any, anyone

ultimus, -a, -um (adj.) last

ultra (adv. and prep.+acc.) more

unde (adv.) whence, wherefore

universus, -a, -um (adj.) all

una cum   together with

unus, -a, -um (num. adj., gen. *unius*) one

usque (adv.) as far as, up to

usus, -us (m.) use

ut (adv. and conj.+subj.) as, in order that

uterque, utraque, utrumque (pron.) each (of two)

utilitas, -tatis (f.) benefit

utor, uti, usus sum (3 dep.+abl.) to use

uxor, -oris (f.) wife

V

vacca, -e (f.) cow

vadio (1) to give security
   vadio legem to pledge one's law (produce compurgators)

vagus, -a (m.f.) tramp, vagrant

vastum, -i (n.) waste

Valentinus, -i (m.) Valentine

vel (conj.) or

vendo, -ere, vendidi, venditum (3) to sell

venella, -e (f.) lane

venerabilis, -e (adj.) venerable

venio, -ire, veni, ventum (4) to come

vere (adv.) truly

veredictum, -i (n.) verdict

vero (adv.) truly

versus (adv. and prep.+acc.) towards, against

verus, -a, -um (adj.) true

via, -e (f.) road, highway

vicarius, -ii (m.) vicar

vicecomes, -itis (m.) sheriff

vicinus, -i (m.) neighbour

video, -ere, vidi, visum (2) to see

vidua, -e (f.) widow

vigilia, -e (f.) eve

villa, -e (f.) town
villanus, -i (m.) villein
vinco, -ere, vici, victum (3) to conquer
vinculum, -i (n.) chain
virga, -e (f.) rod
virgata, -e (f.) virgate
virgo, -inis (f.) virgin
visus, -us (m.) view (of frankpledge)
vita, -e (f.) life
vivarium, -ii (n.) fishpond
vivo, -ere, vixi, victum (3) to live
voco (1) to call
volo, velle, volui to wish
voluntas, -atis (f.) will

vulgus, -i (n. and m.) people, crowd
vulnero (1) to wound
vulnus, -eris (n.) wound

W

Walterus, -i (m.) Walter
warantia, -e (f.) warrant
warantizo (1) to warrant
warda, -e (f.) guardianship
Westmonasterium, -ii (n.) Westminster
Willelmus, -i (m.) William

Y

yems, yemis (f.) winter, also *hiems*

Index of Grammatical Terms

(including references to main illustrative examples)

Select List of Books for Reading
and Further Reference

Latin Dictionaries (Medieval)

Fisher, J.L., *A Medieval Farming Glossary: Latin and English* (National Council of Social Service, 1968)

Harvey, P.D.A. (edit.), *Manorial Records of Cuxham Oxfordshire c.1200-1359* (Hist. Mss. Comm. Joint Publication 23, Oxfordshire Records Society, 1, 1976) contains a glossary of words not found in Latham

Latham, R.E., *Revised Medieval Latin Word-List* (O.U.P. for British Academy, 1965, reprinted 1973). No serious researcher can be without this, which gives numerous variant spellings.

Latin Dictionaries (Classical)

Simpson, D.J., *Cassell's New Compact Latin-English English-Latin Dictionary* (Cassell, 3rd edit. 1966). For research you need a classical as well as medieval dictionary. This is a good dictionary within its compass covering classical Latin to about 100 A.D.

Latin Grammars (Medieval)

Gooder, E.A., *Latin for Local History: an Introduction* (Longmans, 2nd edition 1978). The pioneer modern work.The revised edition includes a brief introduction to palaeography. The word list is very useful for a first quick reference.

Latin Grammars (Classical)

Hendricks, R.A. and Kelly, A.V., *Latin made Simple* (W.H. Allen, 1969). A bright and attractively devised classical grammar for adult students.

Kennedy, B.H., *The Revised Latin Primer* (edited and further revised by J. Mountford, Longmans, 1962). An essential tool for reference, with superb typography and layout.

Special Studies

Alcock, N.W., *Old Title Deeds: a guide for local and family historians* (Phillimore, 1986)

Cheney, C.R., *Handbook of Dates for Students of English History* (Royal Historical Society 1970)

Stuart, D.G., *Manorial Records: an introduction to their transcription and translation* (Phillimore, 1992)

Tarver, A., *Church Court Records: an introduction for family and local historians* (Phillimore, 1995)

Palaeography

Cappelli, A., *Dizionario di Abbreviature Latine ed Italiane* (Hoepli 1985. The explanatory preface is translated by D. Heimann and R. Kay in *The Elements of Abbreviation in Medieval Latin,* Univ. of Kansas Libraries, 1982)

Emmison, F.G., *How To Read Local Archives 1550-1700* (Historical Association 1967)

Hector, L.C., *The Handwriting of English Documents* (Kohler and Coombes facsimile edition, 1980)

Martin, C.T., *The Record Interpreter* (Phillimore, 1982)

Munby, L., *Secretary Hand: a beginner's introduction* (British Association for Local History, 1984)

Munby, L., *Reading Tudor and Stuart Handwriting* (Phillimore for British Association for Local History, 1988)

Newton, K.C., *Medieval Local Records : a Reading Aid* (Historical Association, 1971)

NOTES

NOTES